When A Church Goes Bad

When A Church Goes Bad

by
Casey Sabella

Prescott Press, Inc.
Lafayette, Louisiana

Prescott Press
P.O. Box 53777
Lafayette, LA 70505

Library of Congress Card Catalog Number
92-062152
ISBN 0-933451-08-3

Impreso en Colombia - Printed in Colombia.

DEDICATION

To the many people who made it possible:

Linda Sabella, for her fastidious grammatical editing. Carlene Hill, for arranging my thoughts in such a way as to make sense.

Mike Dowgiewicz, for his counsel, friendship, and encouragement. Tim Tracy together with friends and family for their constructive criticism and input.

And especially to my beloved Patricia, who endured loneliness to allow her husband to spend the hours required to make this book come together. You are still my one and only.

CONTENTS

CONTENTS

PREFACE

Writing is a passion of mine. I have used it to express my thoughts and feelings by keeping a diary of the activity of the Holy Spirit in my life and in my family for several years. *When a Church Goes Bad* began almost accidentally after I had grown weary of the hours and hours of counseling I was giving to Christians who had suffered abuse at the hands of spiritual authority. My original intention was to reduce my workload by writing a small booklet that I could distribute to those needing help. However, when I began, the words flowed, and before long, this booklet was rapidly approaching one hundred pages. I knew then that this project was larger than I anticipated.

Before you read this book, you should know some things. First, I have changed names and certain minor details to protect everyone to whom I refer. The purpose of these accounts is to provide examples of what can and will go wrong in a church that ignores key biblical principles. Whenever appropriate, I have left most of the other information intact to convey the full measure of abuse I experienced under an errant church system. My reason for doing this should become clear by the conclusion of this book.

Secondly, I am flawed. Presenting facts as accurately as I know them has been my aim, and my opinions are those gathered over twenty years of ministry. It is not my intention to be controversial, but to be a catalyst for real change in the Church of Jesus Christ, which I love. Every reader is challenged to measure these thoughts against biblical principles for accuracy and application.

Finally, my ultimate objective is to bring healing to the church. Real health only occurs after sickness has been identified and treated. In essence that means that pain may come first, but the intent is to bring permanent wholeness. My pastor's original vision for ministry was to be a "healer of the breach" in the church, and I am committed to help fulfill that vision.

INTRODUCTION

───────────────────────

  "Give me a *J!*," the pastor shouted.

  "*J!*"

  "Give me an *E!*"

  "*E!*"

  "Give me an *S!*"

  "*S!*"

  "Give me a *U!*"

  "*U!*"

  "Give me another *S!*"

  "*S!*"

  "What's that spell?"

  "*JESUS!*"

  "Louder!"

  "*JESUS!*"

It was a typical Friday night at Good News Chapel, and the hundred or so people stuffed into the small, storefront coffee-house were shouting the "Jesus Cheer" with an enthusiasm to match that of a Super Bowl crowd. The faces in the crowd were young, mostly between thirteen and twenty-five years of age. Some sat around tables—old spools which the phone company had used for wrapping cable and then discarded—others sat shoulder to shoulder on the thinly carpeted floor for this night of praise and celebration, which lasted for two to four hours. Oriental paper shades dimmed the glare from the light bulbs that dangled from the ceiling. Like many others in 1972, these young people were comfortable in places where walls were plastered with psychedelic posters, and the music was rock and roll. Unlike those of their contemporaries however, these posters told of the need to find God, and the music's central message was finding salvation through Jesus Christ.

Between songs, some people raised their hands in the hope of being called upon to share a personal testimony of what Christ had done for them that week. Teen-agers would weep as they told what it was like to live a life blurred by alcohol and drug addiction. Others would tell of the emptiness they found in promiscuous sex. The most important feature of each story was how Jesus had brought lasting peace and satisfaction into their lives. Even parents would come and testify to the phenomenal changes they saw in their sons or daughters.

Near 10 P.M., everyone would begin to smell the aroma brewing in the next room. Closing the meeting in prayer, these "Jesus people" would file out of the main room, grab a coffee and a donut or two, and continue sharing Jesus with the many visitors who had come that night. Sometimes the conversations would go on until midnight. Often, those same visitors could be seen bowing their heads to receive Christ into their lives, as one of the "regulars" led them through the sinner's prayer.

Good News Chapel became the envy of many of the more staid churches in the region because of its effectiveness in reaching people no one else seemed to want: runaways, drug users, alcoholics, and society's drop-outs. Through Good News Chapel, however, young people found a way to God.

Over the next decade, Good News Chapel grew enormously and outreach centers were opened in several communities throughout the state. Thousands of young people encountered Jesus through a gospel preached in the street language of the day. Scores turned from dangerous habits and life-styles to become "new creatures in Christ."

I would never have thought that in time, this anointed ministry, this "cutting edge" church would become an oppressive, cult-like organization. Who would have imagined that this ministry—born in evangelism—would deteriorate to a level in which people's spirituality was judged by how willingly they waxed the pastor's car or how thoroughly they vacuumed the church facility? I never would have believed it—if I hadn't been there.

Good News Chapel was my church. A newborn in Christ when I first walked through the door, Good News Chapel became the central focus of my time and energy for more than fourteen years. I was taught basic Christian doctrine there; I was trained toward leadership and then became a leader there; I met my wife there, and dedicated my first child there. Good News Chapel was my life!

How could such a powerful and dynamic church go so bad? How did I, one of several spiritual leaders, ignore for so many years the dramatic symptoms of decay that were obvious to others outside the church? Why did we help to perpetuate an oppressive system, which would cause so many people deep emotional pain though we knew down deep it was wrong?

This is the story of the struggles I faced when the church I believed in turned sour. It also may be the story of your church, though I hope it is not. I am making an important assumption in sharing this book with you. I am assuming that you did not pick up this book as a weapon to criticize a church to which you have given little of yourself. God knows we don't need more of that. My primary purpose for writing is to help Christians who have given years of their blood, sweat, and tears to a church, only to be devastated by seeming cult-like tendencies in its practices.

My story is not an isolated one. Many churches have been lured into the shipwreck of error by losing their focus on the One who is the Head of the Church. There are churches throughout the world in various stages of demise because they have violated the same biblical principles we did. Some of you have been there, and though you have left, much of your present emotional energy continues to be used up entertaining bitter memories of past hurts. You left, but you haven't quite recovered.

When a Church Goes Bad is a book about pain. We will be looking at the Scriptures to discern what constitutes a church over which Christ is Lord. We will ask important questions designed to cure the spiritual disease of bitterness towards those who hurt you, and then we will examine biblical solutions that will help you back toward spiritual health.

Chapter 1

GOOD NEWS CHAPEL

If you needed proof that God could change a life, you didn't have to look much further than the makeshift pulpit at Good News Chapel. Pastor Mike was a towering figure of a man, standing well over six feet tall and tipping the scales at 260 pounds. He had been a teen-ager in the fifties, when watching Elvis Presley's success made guitar players out of a lot of young men, including Mike. He joined a band, playing nightclubs and bars while looking for the "big break," which never came. He lived life in the fast lane, a single man with seemingly insatiable appetites for wine, women and song—until he met Christine.

Christine was the kind of girl who made a guy like Mike believe he could settle down and become a successful family man. Mike gave it his best shot. He took a "real" job at a used car dealership, where his take-charge nature made him a quick success. Before long he was promoted to general manager. The money began flowing in, but it wasn't long before Christine realized that her new husband hadn't changed much at all. Even Mike's responsibilities as a father did not keep him from his former ways. She was devastated. Within a few short years, their marriage teetered on the brink of divorce.

During this desperate time, Christine heard a local pastor preaching on the radio. She called the number he gave, and soon invited Jesus Christ into her life. One month later, Mike, seeing the changes in his wife, gave himself to Christ as well. Mike's life changed dramatically—so much so that his sales of used cars slumped. Instead of cheating potential customers, he began telling them the truth. Profits plummeted. Other salesmen wondered what had happened to him.

By then, the pastor of the church he was attending had encouraged him to form a gospel band to play special music at worship services. The wife of a nearby Baptist pastor, who had been struck by Mike's zeal for God and ability to relate to young people through music, suggested he visit a notorious discotheque in town to see what God might want to do there. Being the adventurous type, Mike arrived at "THE HOLE IN THE WALL" at midday and discovered a group of streetwise teenage kids using this dilapidated building as their partying hangout.

Mike was bold, sharing Christ with them right then and there. They all gathered around him as he proclaimed that Jesus wanted to utilize their building for His purposes! They agreed to let him use the discotheque on an off-night. Mike challenged these tough street kids to invite their buddies for this special night and left for home amazed at what God had done through him.

Teen-agers came from many of the surrounding towns to hear how this former rock and roller came to know Jesus Christ personally. After hearing his testimony, many responded to the altar call, asking Jesus to change their lives. The teens who managed the discotheque were so impressed with what Mike shared that they invited him to come back week after week. Within a short time, their parents signed the facility over to Mike completely, because they believed that he had a more beneficial plan for its use than their sons had. Mike used it as a Christian coffeehouse for several months, until by order of the local building inspector, it was condemned and eventually torn down.

When I first came to Good News Chapel, the people were meeting in a new location about a mile or so from the original site. The coffeehouse was two-and-one-half-years-old and was growing rapidly. Being seventeen, I felt right at home with these people who were about my age or a little older. There was Jesus, joy, and jeans—plus enough donuts to go around. We tried to do whatever we thought God's will was, preaching on street corners, in parks, in restaurants, and school—virtually anywhere there was a possibility of sharing the gospel.

Good News Chapel wasn't accepted by the rest of the churches in the area, but that never bothered us. In fact, we were probably a little proud of that. The local churches had seldom welcomed hippies and runaways before 1972, why should they start now that we had become a church? This mind-set enabled us to prejudge other Christian groups in the immediate vicinity, thus cutting us off from what might have been godly influences.

Over the next few years, Mike forged the coffeehouse into a more typical church structure. He introduced Sunday morning services and selected elders and deacons from among the congregation, which at that time numbered some 120 people. The Holy Spirit worked in individuals, creating a hunger to serve Christ with an intensity seldom seen in any church. Boys cut their long hair, and girls traded in their miniskirts for more modest attire. Young people, who had been living for their next fix, got off drugs and got jobs in local industries. Our public image became more respectable; although, we remained isolated from other area churches.

After I had served the church for six months, Mike named me a deacon, along with six others. I was shocked and honored at the same time. There was no question that I was dedicated—all church activities took precedence in my calendar. I attended every meeting and participated in every church activity I could . . . but a deacon! And at seventeen-and-one-half-years-old! Looking back, I should have known that something was wrong with this, but the pride of being selected overshadowed any apprehensions I had.

I set out to be the finest deacon possible. Reading every book on the subject (there weren't many), I scrupulously strove to meet every requirement placed before me.

As I finished my senior year of high school, I was at a crossroads. All my life, my father had emphasized the need for me to get a college education. He had put money away for just this purpose. There was also, in my perception, an expectation that I would follow my father in business. All I knew was that I wanted to serve Jesus Christ . . . so much so that I applied only to colleges within driving distance of Good News Chapel.

It was at a special series of meetings held about two hundred miles north of us that God "called" me into the ministry.

Mike had brought several of us with him to help in these special meetings where he was to be the featured speaker. For three evenings in a row, Mike fell flat on his face. It seemed that nothing in his arsenal of sermon materials had any impact on the congregation whatsoever. During the final evening service, perhaps more out of frustration than leading, he called the people forward for individual prayer.

The host pastor joined Mike up front and began praying. When they came to me, he placed his hands upon my head. This man, whom I had never met before, who did not know me from another person off the street, began to tell me things which astounded me. He told me that God was giving him a vision. In it, he saw me teaching God's Word. He told me that God was going to supernaturally empower me to know and to teach the Scriptures. Moments later, as I sat near the altar, God spoke very directly and very surely to me. I did not hear a sound with my ears, nor was there. I could not discern an audible voice, but deep down inside, the words, "You are about to become an elder," registered in my being as clearly as if someone had shouted the words in my ears.

The meeting came to a close, and just as I was ready to dismiss the event as a trick of Satan to puff me up with pride, Mike stopped the benediction with the words, "There's just one more thing we need to do before we close this meeting." Stepping down from the platform, he joined with the other church leaders in telling me that they felt that God had called me to be an elder in the church!

To this day, I remain convinced in my heart that God did indeed choose me to be an elder in Good News Chapel. That belief might seem contradictory, but if you will bear with me, I will attempt to explain myself.

From the moment God spoke that I was to be an elder in Good News, something changed permanently. God began to pour understanding into me far beyond my years or education. I was given the ability to teach the Scriptures as if I had been doing so all my life.

When I returned home, my father and mother were not as exuberant as I. Although my father had given me a "green light" to pursue my future as I wished, his instincts advised me to go to college first. Nevertheless, he consented to allow me to try this direction for six months.

At the ripe old age of eighteen, I began serving Good News Chapel as an elder—full-time. Though I had no training or experience, Pastor Mike allowed me to begin teaching Bible studies and doing light pastoral ministry. God's grace was poured out upon me, as he anointed many of the sermons I would bring from His Word. Looking back on all of this, it scares me.

Before long, I developed a reputation at Good News Chapel for obeying the "boss" no matter what. One of the deacons dubbed me, "Little Mike," a title I did not resist because, in many ways, it fit. I was devoted to implementing whatever directives Pastor Mike issued. My single-mindedness left my peers with the impression that they were dealing with a person who put loyalty to his pastor as the first priority of his life.

As the years went by, other deacons were promoted to eldership responsibilities. A comradeship developed among us which was quite unique. We considered ourselves in a "covenant" relationship with each other, and in some measures we were. We sacrificed together, struggled together, played and prayed and laughed together. We shared meals and whatever else we had. In those early days, none of us had much materially. As a full-time teacher in our day school, my "salary" was

$50 per week, and I learned that I could count on missing ten or twelve checks a year when Mike said that Good News Chapel just didn't have the funds. My attitude stayed positive. "God will provide," I'd say. Somehow or another, I never lacked. I always had, at least, a jar of peanut butter and a loaf of bread.

We had enormous vision and the commitment as a church to match it. We aimed at seeing outreach centers established throughout the state. Thousands were saved through these centers as well as at special conferences held in hotels featuring nationally known Christian leaders. We came to believe that our ministry would be God's special vessel to turn people back to God—but we were doomed.

Unfortunately, the unraveling of our ministry matches the pattern of many churches today. The seeds of pride were planted deeply into the soil of Good News. These seeds of destruction would blossom eventually and choke the life out of the other fruit the church produced. Pride was watered with unchecked authority and fertilized with a severe lack of accountability. As the church grew, it looked healthy from afar, but soon its poisonous fruit would destroy many of the young believers who had trusted it to provide nourishment.

Our church went bad gradually. It is said that you can boil a frog alive provided you turn up the heat slowly while it sits in a pot of water. The frog will adapt its body temperature until it is unknowingly cooked to death. (If you attempted to throw a frog into a pot of already boiling water, he would immediately "feel" the danger and do everything to escape.) Like the frog, many of us didn't recognize the spiritual temperature until it was too late.

Looking back, I can see clearly now that our church's problems began to surface when Good News Chapel purchased a tract of farm land from one of the members. The church, we were told, would use the existing house on the property to provide a live-in center for young men who were given the choice between juvenile detention centers or us. Contacts were mainly to come through referral from social workers or relatives.

Pledges were taken, and work began on the old house to make it suitable for its future occupants. Thousands of dollars were raised, and more thousands were committed to make this dream a reality.

Then a different reality surfaced. Mike announced to the congregation that his family would move into the new house, and an additional building would be constructed for the center. No one opposed providing for Mike's family, because everyone realized that Mike had sacrificed much through the years, living in a cramped duplex with four growing children. Although everyone wanted to see Mike and his family blessed with a new place to live, the process he used to acquire it left a bad taste in everyone's mouth.

Long-time members began murmuring among themselves about the ethics of this sudden change of plans. As one of five elders at the time, I had to wonder myself, but there was no clear process to appeal any of Mike's decisions.

Hearing that criticism was circulating around the church, Mike announced at a subsequent service that God had told him to move into the house, and for those who disagreed, it was just too bad! A few days later, he moved his family into the newly refurbished facility. He had rammed "God's will" down our throats, but he refused to allow others to enter the process of discerning what God's will was. The events surrounding the purchase and utilization of that farm land sent a clear signal to everyone that Mike's word was infallible.

Still, we felt powerless to challenge him. The only system we had for challenging a decision was direct confrontation. Mike was well over six feet tall, with a deep, booming voice that made the squeamish wish they had never spoken. If you confronted Mike on any issue, it usually cost you—not only then, but in time to come. Mike was not a man who easily forgave those who opposed him.

On several occasions, people less close to Mike suggested a more viable system of accountability. Each suggestion met total resistance from Mike. He, after all, "built the church" from the ground up. He would often counter someone with, "Who are you to question?" or, "What gives you the right to challenge my authority?" Reactions like these helped to prevent people from making appropriate and godly appeals.

Adding to all this was Mike's health. Coinciding with his move into the church's newly renovated facility, he began a bout with a hereditary disease, which would require constant medical attention. In effect, Mike remained sick for the next nine years, and his illness made biblical accountability that much more elusive.

You see, no one wants to confront a sick man. No one wants to be the one who brings more stress into an already stressful situation. We cared for Mike, and we prayed for him and his family constantly during this extended period of trial. All-night prayer vigils and days of fasting were conducted to seek a healing miracle from God. At the same time, however, many church members resented the fact that this illness enabled him to wield more and more absolute power because of the sympathy his sickness engendered.

Mike's lack of biblical training paved the way for him to misuse Scripture. Old Testament models of absolute leadership by a divinely appointed individual seemed to drive home his "right" to lead as he saw fit. He completely ignored the New Testament model of the servant leader, which might have helped him form a network among pastors of other fellowships, or which might have even given him ears to hear our legitimate concerns.

Gradually, Mike began to overemphasize the authority of leaders and the necessity of submission to them. Unquestioned obedience to authority developed into the ultimate test of faith. I actually remember Mike telling me, at a time when he and I disagreed: "Listen, when I say 'jump', you say, 'How high?'" The sort of leadership allegiance and loyalty expected by this command was total in scope. If Mike determined that the course of action for my life was to turn left, then I was not to question; I was to obey, believing that God was using him as a direct agent of guidance.

Underemphasis of authority can also be a problem in today's churches, though it wasn't the case with us. Some congregations disregard the authority and anointing of church leaders to such a degree that the pastor or elders become pawns in the hands of an ambitious church board. This is equally reprehensible and has its own set of disastrous consequences, which I mention only in passing since it is not our focus.

Mike was a zealous leader with no formal training. Subsequently, he had little regard for it in my ministry as well. He was an immature leader guiding an immature leader. In retrospect, most of us can discern that it is unwise to place a boy of eighteen into the role of elder in a church, but how do we deal with the fact that God seemed to be the agent who made the decision?

God did in fact call me to be an elder. However, when church leaders are not mature, they mistake calling with separation, and these are two entirely different processes. Paul the apostle was called on the road to Damascus, but he was separated by the elders in his home church of Antioch many years later.

At Good News Chapel, none of us had understanding as to how to implement what the Holy Spirit was saying. We were immature, because we were isolated and unaccountable. When God spoke clearly that I was to be an elder, Mike acted on that word. However, we all failed to seek to understand what the process was. If God said the same thing to a boy of twelve, would we immediately ordain him? Of course not!

While God did anoint me to teach, in retrospect it would have been a wiser move on the part of the church to appoint a man with a call to ministry. As I developed in character and wisdom, it might have been appropriate then to separate me to serve as an elder in the congregation. Our lack of spiritual maturity merged calling and separation, forcing us to miss some steps in God's process of raising up biblical leadership.

We unconsciously had come to feel that our church was so superior to all others, that we were so outstanding, that we were such an elite new generation of Christians who were different from all others—that we could be convinced that our leaders had a heavenly hotline. We had come to accept that disobeying our leaders was tantamount to directly disobeying God.

The seeds of power abuse continued to grow stronger and to bear more and more bitter fruit. People thought that by serving the pastor's needs, we were serving Christ. Because of his ever-increasing control over people's decisions, we became extremely dependent on Mike for direction. With that, the need to win Mike's approval became crucial. When I began pastoring one of our daughter churches, I continued to depend upon Mike for spiritual decisions. His involvement in my church was all-consuming.

One way the need for approval from Mike manifested itself was on the men's faces. Mike wore a beard, and so did 75 percent of the men who belonged to Good News Chapel! Is there anything wrong with imitating a church leader? Not at all. In our church, however, a type of peer pressure developed that made the clean shaven feel like they were not part of the "inner circle." Anyone willing to acknowledge the obvious would see the same approval-seeking pattern in the church parking lot. Not less than fifteen Buick Cutlass Supremes of various colors could be counted among perhaps seventy-five cars. Mike had three; the elders each had one . . . do you get the picture? Individuals wanted Mike's approval so badly that they would go out of their way to take care of whatever needs he might have. People waxed his car, bought him special gifts, gave him expensive Christmas presents—even gave him monthly love offerings—in addition to their regular church offering—all to please him in concrete ways.

As we tried to prove ourselves worthy of his approval, we even began to spy on and report on other members. Those loyal to Mike became "scouts." Anyone in the church membership who acted in a way we knew to be contrary to Good News Chapel's policy would be reported directly to him. As bizarre as this seems to a normal Christian, those operating under such a system are like the frog in warm water. They do not perceive that there is anything terribly wrong.

Even the church elders vied for his approval. I would betray my fellow elders on any level if I saw them violate our unwritten and arbitrary rules and regulations. Mike would use us to inform on each other if it served his purpose. A very real sense of paranoia developed, in which everyone in authority watched everyone else.

To give you the full-blown picture of what our ministry became, look at the condition of our church just before the sudden death of the pastor. Each member was expected to travel up to 120 miles round trip to attend each of three church meetings per week. No excuses were acceptable. Those who missed church events were either privately confronted or left to squirm in their seats during sermons that chastised "those who don't."

Deacons and elders were expected to devote their Saturdays doing maintenance at the church-owned farm where Mike lived. We mowed lawns, painted, did repairs, vacuumed, washed floors, and even shoveled manure off the fields into a designated pile so that, clearing the land of unsightly cow flops, the property would be a better witness to the community. Anyone who hoped to become a leader adjusted his schedule accordingly.

It had started innocently enough. When we first purchased the farm, certain skilled members were asked to volunteer their time to help construct fencing or make repairs. Over time, this volunteerism deteriorated into mandatory "work days." There is nothing wrong with church members pitching in to help in the physical needs of any ministry. Thank God for people who care enough to do so! In our case, however, these chores were expected of us. We did not volunteer. Many of us left lawns at home unmowed, houses with leaky faucets, etc., so we could fulfill our "responsibility" to see to it that the church property maintained its "witness to the community."

All full-time workers were severely underpaid. College educated, state-certified teachers were given minimum wage paychecks. It was not unusual for each member of the paid staff to be expected to give back ten to twelve paychecks per year due to lack of funds. Yet, church-owned livestock were fed the best of hay and grain. The pastor and his family owned the finest cars, wore the latest fashions, and enjoyed all the benefits of wealth. Sacrifice is a very real part of Christian ministry. Sometimes a church simply cannot afford to compensate staff adequately in its early stages. Good News Chapel failed to care for their key people, choosing instead to maintain an image of wealth in the community. Staff members scraped and clawed to meet the pressing needs of housing, clothing, and food.

All leaders were expected to purchase and wear clothing with our children's ministry emblem printed boldly on the front. Its ludicrous design made the most dignified person look like a clown. On Bible study nights, our church would be filled with people wearing bright-yellow t-shirts with a smiling penguin on the front, together with our church name. Leaders who did not wear this clothing would be angrily confronted by Mike. (On one occasion, I wore a jacket with this shirt and was summarily "chewed out" because the jacket covered part of the emblem.)

All offerings from our network of four churches were delivered to the central office. Each local assembly was not permitted to exercise any control over how its monies were spent. Only a select few had any opportunity to review the financial records of our church at all, and they did not have the authority to change any policies whatsoever. As pastor of one of the congregations, I didn't even have the right to buy letterhead for my church. Requests for such needs were oftentimes trivialized as unneeded, or they were deferred due to more pressing needs.

What were some of those pressing needs? Saddles and headgear for the many horses (most of which fulfilled their entire purpose by eating hay), an above-ground pool purchased for the teen-agers, bi-yearly painting of existing buildings, which already looked better than any other facility in the community, a pony cart for recreational rides around the property, fencing for the livestock, the construction of storage buildings, which remained 90 percent empty—essentially, any item that enhanced the operation of the central headquarters.

The single advantage of the central headquarters being responsible for all church expenditures was that new congregations would not have to worry about meeting the basic expenses of rent and utilities. While it was true that there was a big advantage to this arrangement at the outset, the flip side was that for a long while after a given congregation became self-supporting, it remained fully dependent on the "mother" church. Growth was impossible. "Daughter" churches didn't even have control over the religious art on their own walls. When the central church was putting the finishing touches on its new building, Mike decided that the gold cross hanging on the wall in another of our churches would look better in the new building! The cross, which had hung there for years, simply disappeared one Sunday morning and reappeared in the central church. No matter what we felt, we all mouthed agreement that it looked much better in the new church building than it did in its former home.

These events are indeed unbelievable—yet they occurred. If some of you have witnessed similar abuses taking place in your fellowship, read on. By God's grace, you will begin to see a difference between a church built on the solid rock of Jesus Christ and a church built on the backs of its members' efforts, to the glory of the pastor or other leaders. Knowing the difference will save you or a loved one years of unnecessary heartache.

Chapter 2

A CHURCH WITH PROBLEMS
—OR A PROBLEM CHURCH ?

You've seen a few things going on in your church that you aren't exactly crazy about. There have been decisions implemented which seemingly have done more to help the leadership look good than to meet the spiritual needs of the congregation. People outside of Christ are not impressed with the way your church communicates the power and love of Christ. You have spoken to church authorities about the way they do things, but have met with overwhelming resistance.

The question now surfaces: Are you dealing with a church which seems to have a few problems that can be worked through, or are you dealing with a problem church to which you need to say, . . . "Good-bye"?

There are eight areas we need to examine closely to assess your church's spiritual condition. And no matter what the leadership tells you, it *is* your business!

First, is your church *financially accountable*? It may seem crass to put money at the top of a list when determining the spiritual health of a church, but you will find that unhealthy churches tend to have unhealthy policies about their use of funds.

A financial expert once told me that he believed he could determine the health of a business by how ethically its finances were managed. If the business mismanaged money, other aspects of the company were also mismanaged. He would find evidence of disregarded company policies, misuse of executive privileges, abuse of employees, communication problems, and a host of other inequities. What he said in passing had a great impact upon me, since I knew that my church at that time was extremely unethical in its financial dealings.

To be fair, not all ministries with financial inequities are necessarily crooks and false prophets. Ministers are normally trained in theology, not business administration (unfortunately). There are churches that have been overwhelmed with numerical growth and were not prepared for it. That does not mean they are evil. They need help, not criticism.

What I am referring to is the deliberate evasion by leaders to discuss how monies are collected and utilized. If simple questions are answered by, "Don't worry about it," WORRY ABOUT IT!

To date, I have yet to see a church become cultic that has not fallen down in its methods of finance. The correct use of money is a barometer of other things as well. Jesus said, ". . . So if you have . . . not been trustworthy in handling worldly wealth, who will trust you . . . with true riches?" (Luke 16:11).

Our Lord uses a person's attitude toward money and use of money as a gauge to discern faithfulness in ministry. A leader who is not careful with the monies entrusted to his care by God, tends to be careless with the souls entrusted to his care as well. If he has found ways to manipulate church finances to his own personal advantage, he will probably find ways to manipulate church members to his own personal advantage, too.

The funds given to a church are being donated to God's work. Church leaders are stewards of these funds. I believe strongly that leaders should be properly remunerated for their work. Too many pastors suffer at the hands of stingy church boards who are dedicated to keeping the pastor "humble" by forcing him to deliver pizzas on the side to make ends meet. That is wrong by any standard. On the other hand, the purpose of giving is not meant to help those in ministry enjoy the life-styles of the rich and famous.

There needs to be a fair means of evaluating and meeting the needs of those whose livelihood is the church.

Any church member would do well to consider the processes used by their church for collection, distribution, and investment of donated monies. Questions to ask might include:

—How are decisions about spending made?

—Do members have access to information about how funds are distributed with respect to the financial needs of each individual? Is there evidence that the pastor has to scratch for money because of a meager salary?

—Is one leader living high on the hog, while his fellow staff member has a working wife and a twelve-year-old Buick?

Many of you reading this think that an approach like this is very bold—perhaps so. But would you rather spend valuable years of your life investing your time and money into a church only to learn it has been deliberately mismanaged for personal advantage?

In churches that become cultic, such questions as the above can be very threatening. The one asking may be made to feel that they do not trust those in leadership. It has become my view that those in a position of trust are required to demonstrate when they should be trusted. The proper use of funds is the most basic trust a church gives to its leadership. How finances are spent and the method of accountability used is a clear signal as to the health of the church. And even the healthiest churches ought to demonstrate their willingness to be held accountable in financial matters. When a minority keep financial matters secret, look for a power-based leadership. The way is paved for cultic behavior.

A second sign might be posed as a question: What is the *appeal process* used in your church to settle disputes? In other words, what happens if church leadership begins making unscriptural decisions? How and to whom do you as a member appeal?

In many churches, a member may approach the board of elders when questioning the words or actions of a pastor. These churches have written into their constitution that the pastor is accountable to the elders and that they have the authority to bring corrective discipline. A written policy as to why and how this takes place is vital to the survival of any church.

How does the leadership in your church respond when challenged? To avoid accountability, power-based leaders surround themselves with non-confrontational men. In the business world, we would call them "yes men." Their function is primarily to listen to decisions the leader has already made and add their rubber stamp of approval. Those who do dare to challenge will usually be labeled and removed. In churches, these non-confrontational leaders will strive to enforce the pastor's directives, not out of the conviction that these directives are anointed by God, but out of fear of confrontation.

I look back in shame today at the things I "approved" by silence through my years under Mike's leadership. Had I studied the Scriptures properly, I would have seen that elders are appointed by God to conduct the affairs of the church. I would have seen that leadership is designed to work as a team, not a dictatorship. Leaders who serve with the pastor are to hear from God as well, confirming or challenging decisions based upon principles from God's word irrespective of whether anyone likes it. Confrontation is not always an evil thing. It can be a means through which leaders "sharpen" each other.

Manipulative pastors, however, will utilize a wide array of emotional outbursts to secure control over confronters. One way is by yelling down such opponents. Interestingly, Proverbs 25:28 tells us: "Like a city whose walls are broken down, is a man who lacks self-control." When applied to the church context, we see that a church is open to enemy attack when the leader repeatedly deals with opposition through hostility and anger.

Through the years, Mike and I had knock-down, drag-out arguments. Both of us left these experiences more wounded than when we started. I regret that I did not follow the Matthew 18:15-18 procedure to either see problems dealt with scripturally or else resign with a clear conscience. Leaders of churches are not commissioned by their Lord to "play dead." Leaders are reminded by Hebrews 13:17 that they must give account of church members before God. This fear ought to wake us up so that we realize we cannot be part of manipulative church government and pretend innocence.

Ask yourself:

—What is the formal or informal appeal process in your church? If the pastor errs, who jumps in to bring order and direction to the church? Ideally, this should be written somewhere to avoid confusion.
—How is true repentance measured?
—Do you know of any instance when the pastor or other leaders have ever publicly repented when confronted with wrongdoing?

A spirit of repentance needs to characterize all God's people.

Another factor you need to consider in determining your church's spiritual condition: Does your church have its *own language* designed to obscure what is really going on? Let's borrow a good dictionary definition of what I call "mumbo-jumbo:" "Language or ritualistic activity that is intended to confuse" (*American Heritage Dictionary, Second College Edition*).

Since rediscovering Christianity, I have helped those entrapped in the teaching of the Jehovah's Witnesses. Through an outreach of our church, we provide the information they need to examine the Watchtower and to convert to Christianity. When the Holy Spirit attracted me to help these individuals, I began an in-depth study of how this particular cult operated. What I learned scared me. Many of the confusing techniques of mind control that they regularly use on their membership were similar if not altogether identical to what I had experienced in Good News Chapel.

Let me clarify: Most Jehovah's Witnesses do not intentionally practice mind control. They are for the most part sincere, dedicated people. However, through following the direction of leaders who follow the direction of their leaders, all Jehovah's Witnesses end up practicing mind control whether deliberately or in ignorance. Jehovah's Witnesses, for example, are not allowed to read any literature that speaks of their church organization in a disparaging way. Further, they are taught that the *Watchtower* magazine is the sole channel through which God speaks to people today—in addition to the Bible. All other churches are considered satanic. Leaving their organization is the same to them as leaving God.

Fear rules the minds and therefore the lives of Jehovah's Witnesses. They are terrified of being separated from this organization for fear of being rejected by God. Questioning the society's past or present dealings leads to being put on trial by the leaders at the local Kingdom Hall. Taught to trust leadership implicitly, Jehovah's Witnesses never give a thought to the notion that they are under the influence of cult mind control.

In the Watchtower organization, as in other cultic organizations, members develop their own "mumbo-jumbo" when referring to commonly used words. When a normal person refers to "Christendom" for example, he is speaking of the vast collection of different expressions of Christianity. When the Jehovah's Witness refers to Christendom, he means demonically inspired people who claim the name *Christian*, but who are really God's enemies. All non-Jehovah's Witnesses who attend other churches fit into this category. In a similar way, when a Jehovah's Witness refers to being "in the truth," he does not mean honest and upright. He means actively serving the Watchtower organization, which is equal in their minds to serving God Himself. If you are referred to as "inactive," this does not denote that you are sluggish or ill. To be inactive means that you do not knock on doors or participate in doing what they consider vital to serving Jehovah's organization. Therefore, an "inactive person" is a "weak" brother or sister. Others may be labeled "worldly" if they drive a new car or have expensive items in their home.

Use of such "mumbo jumbo" keeps the rank and file Witness in line with the objectives of the Watchtower society. Out of fear of being labeled, the Jehovah's Witness will think twice before seeking information from sources other than the cult itself. Fear of being considered "an apostate"—someone who violates Watchtower rules—binds many into an eternal destiny without Christ.

A manipulative leader uses "mumbo jumbo" to control members much the same way the Watchtower uses it to control Jehovah's Witnesses. These words are so common to those in the church, that they have adopted them unknowingly into their everyday language. Sometimes a group of churches share this same lingo. There can develop an air of superiority about using these words as part of conversation.

At Good News Chapel, we labeled people "rebellious to God" if they did not submit themselves to the myriad of unspoken rules and regulations we had. We allowed little room for anyone to question decisions we made. In effect, that meant that we considered ourselves infallible, though we never made that claim. The behavior determining rebellion was obvious to us. Anyone not giving absolute allegiance to our decisions as leaders was branded with the "R" word.

Synonyms for "rebellious" used in other churches might be an "unsubmitted," "maverick," or "independent spirit." All these labels are designed to isolate individual members into classifications that can be used against them should they leave the church. The issue is seldom rebellion in the biblical sense of the word. The real issue is whether a church member is willing to put aside his or her conscience and submit to leadership out of personal loyalty.

Certainly we do not deny that there are saints who demonstrate a tendency towards rebellion against God-ordained authority. People need to be taught to have a proper relationship with those in spiritual authority (Rom. 13:1; Heb. 13:17). However, when a pastor is not accountable to anyone and wishes to keep it that way, it is amazing how he can turn the attention away from his own deficiency by labeling others "rebellious" for not saying "Amen" to every decision he makes.

Rebellion is the unwillingness of any individual to listen to or receive direction from God. Sun Myung Moon exercises authority, but I am unwilling to listen to or receive direction from him. That does not make me rebellious. Rebellion only becomes an issue when an individual violates what the Bible clearly states.

For example, if my pastor, who carries spiritual authority from God tells me to stop practicing adultery, I am obligated as a child of God to listen to and obey his counsel. If I disregard that counsel, I am living in rebellion. He is the human object of my rebellion, but God is the one against whom I am truly rebelling. On the other hand, if that same pastor tells me to break off my relationship with another Christian because he no longer attends our church, I may refuse without being rebellious. He is asking me to submit to counsel that has no basis in God's Word.

Rebellion is measured by a person's response to God's Word. Our primary focus as leaders is not to identify who is and who is not a rebel, but to lead the flock of God by our example. Individuals may resist commitment to the church for a variety of reasons, and leaders need to be sensitive to that.

Recently, a woman I will call Jean had the unique task of "baby-sitting" a small flock of sheep for a week. During a newscast, a weather report was issued predicting a hurricane by mid-day. It was already raining when Jean anxiously sprang into action. She attempted to gather the sheep into the barn to protect them from harm, but to no avail. They simply could not be persuaded to come in out of the rain. After two frustrating hours of chasing sheep, Jean called John, a next-door neighbor, to help her out of this dilemma. John came and reassured her that everything would be fine. He encouraged Jean to go inside and dry off, while he rounded up the flock.

To her complete amazement, Jean watched as John lured the sheep into the barn. By using a little grain and by standing reasonably still, all but one came in out of the rain. The last sheep would not respond, however. Jean thought to herself, "What a rebellious sheep! Doesn't it realize that John is only trying to help?" She thought of the spiritual application: How many of God's sheep are running away from Him when He is only trying to help them? Finally, this last sheep was secured, and John stopped inside to dry himself off. Jean shared her new-found biblical application with John from the actions of the sheep that had gone astray. John looked at her quizzically and said, "That sheep was not rebellious—it was just scared when it couldn't find the others."

Rebellion against God's standards is a serious offense, which needs to be dealt with using biblical principles in a spirit of humility. Oftentimes, however, we are not dealing with rebellion. Like the sheep that has gone astray, we are dealing with someone who is frightened or confused. If we judge them rebellious or unsubmissive due to their lack of commitment to church functions, we can miss the mark and fail to help them benefit from God's grace.

One label used more than any other I know of today to silence the influence of women in the church is Jezebel. This label can be one of the more insidious and harmful examples of "mumbo jumbo" a leader uses to manipulate church members.

Historically, Jezebel was one of the most wicked women who ever lived. She dominated her husband and worshiped false gods instead of the true God (1 Kings 16:30-34). She murdered prophets and, with the consent of Ahab, ruled Israel through witchcraft and intimidation. Her reputation brought God's angry wrath, and she was judged severely.

In Revelation, Jesus accuses a woman in the Thyatira church of being a spiritual Jezebel. That woman was also judged severely by Him for her lack of repentance. Christ himself sentenced her to death along with those who followed her. Using these two texts of Scripture, a number of churches have warned us extensively to beware of the Jezebels of our day.

I have no doubt that there are people today whose actions exactly imitate those of Jezebel. I also have no doubt that in the church of Jesus Christ there are certain women who manifest a spirit of control over their own husbands and families, thus hindering the work of God. Being aware of women who manipulate men, and properly dealing with them, is a correct practice.

Ironically, however, the manipulative leader can use the label "Jezebel" to frighten off all would-be opposition. Jezebel notwithstanding, God does speak to and through women. Women in general have been equipped by God with an intuitive sense that is designed by him to help the church. Women are usually first to sense that leadership is going the wrong way. Men do not traditionally pay as much attention to detail as women do. It is in the little things that we often discover the bigger picture. Women (collectively) are equipped to spot the little things that have meaning.

My wife is not by nature a critical person. If she gets a "bad feeling" about an individual, I do not ignore it. It is not her disposition to have bad feelings about anyone. When we were newlyweds, I did ignore these intuitive observations and suffered greatly for it. I learned over the years to pray about my wife's insights, for often God is using her as my helpmate to rescue me out of unseen danger.

There are individual women who are misguided, self-appointed leaders who need to be scripturally dealt with. However, when the majority of women in any given church are concerned about how things are said and done, let me assure you: There is a real problem! The controlling leader effectively destroys many women by publicly or privately referring to them as "Jezebels." In doing so, he effectively silences the ability of that woman to sound any concern over how things are being done in the church. If a husband listens to his wife, then he is "following Jezebel." The "J" word becomes a tool to destroy all women who would oppose wrong decisions. Women are permanently labeled in the community, and the counsel of God through them is nullified.

Each church group, movement, or denomination tends to have its own lingo. When you think about it, some of the phrases we as Christians have become accustomed to could be construed as bizarre to the outsider. We speak about not wanting to be "of the world," or about being blessed because we are "washed in the blood." Do we mean that we want to live on Mars? Do we take baths in red liquid? Of course not. The difference between this type of "Christianese" and "mumbo jumbo" is that the latter is purposefully using words to gain personal advantage. "Mumbo jumbo" metes out harsh judgment by labeling those who oppose absolute authority. What language is spoken at your church?

  —Do church members use labels that serve to brand certain individuals or groups as less spiritual?

—Are the women of the church able to communicate
their concerns without being ostracized?
—Do newcomers have a difficult time understanding
the language of your church? Is the simple message of
the gospel being obscured by mumbo jumbo that ema-
nates from the pulpit?

Another sign of trouble in any church is *isolation of the
pastor*. We are not designed by God to be isolated parts of a
body. We are designed to be a part of one another. Within the
church, it is easy for the pastor to become isolated. People
expect much from him. He feels he must meet their expectations, desires, hopes, dreams, goals, and needs. He cannot.
Only God can, and the pastor needs to resist the urge to assume
responsibilities for which God has not graced him.

Because of unbalanced teaching through the centuries, we
have come to accept an unrealistic separation between clergy
and laity. The Bible recognizes no such division. We all have
different gifts, but we are equal with respect to our participa-
tion in the Church. Jesus told his disciples that if they wanted to
lead, they would have to be the best servants. Few ministers
believe that. Most have been taught through magazines, books,
and schooling that the most polished speakers are the best
leaders, or that the most dynamic personalities are the best. So
many pastors strive to be honored among their peers, and by so
doing, lose their human frailty—an essential characteristic of a
good leader.

Pastors, like everyone else, need friends. Ideally, they should
have friends inside the church and outside the church. It is
amazing to me that seminaries spend so much time pumping
students with theology and church growth principles, but so
little time training them to serve people. Pastors are driven to
build big churches in order to discover self-worth. What is the
result? Isolation. Isolation breeds dictators who do not know
how to work with others. Healthy friendships destroy isolation.
The book of Proverbs records for us some of the value of
friendships:

> A friend loves at all times, and a brother is born for
> adversity. (17:17)

Wounds from a friend can be trusted, but an enemy multiplies kisses. (27:6)

Perfume and incense bring joy to the heart, and the pleasantness of one's friend springs from his earnest counsel. (27:9)

As iron sharpens iron, so one man sharpens another. (27:17)

It is evident from these Scriptures and others that God uses friendships to give us his counsel and direction. So many church leaders lack direction because they are isolated. Authority does not originate from doing a job perfectly. Nor does it come from a graven image of spirituality. Authority comes from the Father and is confirmed to others by Him. We should not be afraid of making mistakes. We should be afraid of not confessing them to others when we do.

Through the counsel of a close friend, we made a change in our church recently. We dropped the use of the "pastor" title from my name. I am not saying this is right for you, or that to be on the cutting edge you need to do this. For our church, the title "pastor" in front of my name made me a little more distant and a little too central to the church in general.

Now please understand: I have been called "pastor" for years. But as another pastor said to his congregation, "You can call me 'Pastor Ken' when I can call you 'Electrician Bob' or 'Secretary Sally.'" The point he was making was that pastor is a function more than a title.

When we instituted this change in our fellowship, I didn't lose my authority. People joked about it a bit. But people do not treat me like a nobody because I dropped the title. In fact, the respect level of our congregation for our pastoral team might have increased as lay people see leadership striving to remove every potential obstacle for their spiritual growth and development.

Some still call me "pastor." That is fine. I call others by that title if it means something to them. I am not trying to tear down a particular church tradition. I am simply affirming that authority from God does not come by creating an image of spirituality.

People in our congregations need to know that the pastor has friends to whom he can go. I believe they want that.

Friendships develop over time and at different levels. Pastors need the kind of friendships where they can be vulnerable. This is no small challenge. The average pastor in America strives to find his identity in a bigger and better church. In the environment of competition with his peers, there is little room for vulnerability—yet without it, he will most certainly fall.

A leader, like everyone else, needs people around him who are not flattering or exalting him into something he never was or was meant to be. He needs people he can trust to "wound" him, knowing that they are doing so because they care. Leaders need good counsel and conflict at times. When "iron sharpens iron" two people get sharp. I believe that it is high time the Body of Christ moves away from being so dull!

Conversely, a pastor does not need people who challenge every decision he makes. Trust must be given. No pastor excels when people are breathing down his neck almost every moment. A pastor needs people to recreate with, to "let his hair down" with, to go fishing with, and so on. The congregation needs to accept him as a man called by God, yet still a man.

Ideally, the leaders within a church ought to be friends. One brother in Christ challenged me by asking, "If these men were not elders in your church, would they still be your friends?" In other words, is your relationship with other leaders based primarily on how well they perform tasks, or upon how much you genuinely care for them as individuals? It was because I could not answer "yes" that I began to reexamine my relationship with these men.

For a pastor/leader, a great safeguard against deception is to develop friendships inside the church and with leaders from other churches. What value is it, after all, if there are twenty-five born-again churches in a given region, and no one pastor truly cares about any of the others? Will God want to fully bless any of those churches? I doubt it. By meeting each other on the golf course, a tennis court, or for lunch, church leaders begin to know each other and entrust themselves to the care of each other. Out of these relationships, good counsel comes. Good prayer for each others' needs comes. Out of these relationships, iron sharpens iron. Out of these relationships, the Body of Christ grows in a region, and leaders are protected from pride and arrogance.

The best type of accountability outside the local church comes from deep, biblically based friendships. Isolated leaders are easy targets for false teaching. They develop into desperate men who commit stupid errors, which affect innocent people. Let's face it: God never intended for leaders to do the whole job of bringing their entire region to Christ. Ministers are a part of the whole, so why not acknowledge that and connect with others? In the long run, God's vision for each person's church will be helped, not hindered, by linking together with others.

Isolation is not just a problem with the pastor. Whole congregations can experience the same problem, resulting in spiritual pride, which sends churches skidding towards cultism. When the membership believes they are just a little more spiritual, or a little more knowledgeable than other churches in town, watch out! This pride can invade a church through a number of means. Perhaps the congregation has grown larger and faster than other area congregations. Members may begin thinking that the growth their church enjoys is God's way of telling them, "I approve of your church the most." People become proud of the abundance or scope of programs the church offers, or the percentage of income given to the church, or the number of people on staff, or the speed with which those who won't "get with the program" are removed from the group. Churches that intentionally isolate themselves from other born-again churches are often guilty of spiritual pride. This usually begins with the leadership but can become the predominant spirit of the members.

What signs indicate isolation in the pastor?

—Does he and his family always look "stressed?"
—Does the pastor relax among people, or do you always get a sense that he is "on"?
—Do you know whether the pastor has close friends either inside or outside of the church?

—Are you aware of the pastor's weaknesses? Did you learn what they were from him, from friends, from enemies, or by circumstances? Is there a strong effort to minimize these weaknesses, and even to pretend they do not exist?

—Do parishioners speak down to others, as if they were spiritually immature for attending elsewhere?

—Is the pastor/leader's name mentioned an unusually disproportionate number of times as compared with the mention of the name of Jesus?

"Pride," the Scripture says "goes before destruction, a haughty spirit before a fall" (Prov. 16:18). While Christians testify the world over about God's deliverance from sinful habits, let us not fall prey to the sin that ejected Lucifer from Heaven. It is not a minor sin.

Another disease sure to destroy the health of your church is the *tendency to disregard principles from the Bible.* There is trouble down the road for congregations that ignore violations of the character traits required of a leader in I Timothy 3:1-7. Men come into ministry by meeting these requirements, and it is assumed that they remain qualified for life. In actuality, these standards can become lax if not diligently maintained. And, when the standards do become lax, the church suffers.

Does the pastor/leader continue to meet the standards of I Timothy 3:1-7? Who holds him accountable to these standards? Is he above reproach? Self-controlled? Is there evidence that the home is managed well? Do his children respect his authority? Does he practice hospitality? Is he approachable? What kind of moral standards does he demonstrate? Our objective here is not to create unrealistic criticism, since we all have faults, but to discern whether the standards Paul initiated by the Holy Spirit are being implemented or minimized as irrelevant.

Some leaders have made a god out of the office of pastor. Men can become so enamored with the prestige and personal benefits of this office that they become entrenched in protecting a calling that is a gift from God. There are a lot of benefits to leading a church. Pastors gain respect in the community. They are aware that God has chosen them for important work. They get affirmation from a congregation that loves them. Hopefully, these are not the reasons why most people would enter the ministry, but they are benefits to church leaders.

When there is little accountability in a given congregation, additional benefits might include a hefty salary, the ability to change the church to fit one's own tastes, the undisputed authority to make decisions, and the power to install staff members who agree, or to remove staff members who disagree.

Because of these potential benefits, some leaders tend to deify their position, feeling that they are pastor for life. Any suggestion of change from other leaders is often met with swift rebuke. I suppose I have heard the Scripture about God's gifts and callings being without repentance a billion times. What I seldom hear when discussing a current leader's failures are the standards of I Timothy 3:1-7. God put I Timothy 3:1-7 in his Word to inform us about his standards for leaders. Careful consideration of these passages indicate that it is entirely possible during the course of one's ministry to become disqualified. Take, for example, the problem of a church leader whose children become openly disobedient to his authority. Following the scriptural pattern, the elder or church leader needs to step down from leadership and focus all of his energies on his family's needs. The majority of leaders today would be horrified at the thought. But which is better: the welfare of the family and the upholding of the Word of God, or the continuity of a leader's image?

I know of one man who spent many years on the mission field. While there, he began to have marriage problems, and his wife took his two daughters and returned home. He stayed on, no doubt with the idea of sacrificing his family to continue the ministry God had called him to establish. Today, that ministry numbers in the hundreds of thousands—at least for now. But, marriages in the ministry's leadership are, by all accounts, just as insidiously terrible as that of the founder. Though this man can point to numbers "saved," the real fruit is a lack of regard for marriages and families. God's hand of judgment is already working to bring this "ministry" to destruction. It does not represent Christ's interests any longer.

Before leaving the issue of biblical issues, is there evidence of *doctrinal error*? Those who have been members of the same group for a number of years become accustomed to its various nuances and quirks. Some are insignificant but others are important.

Through the years I have known of several churches that have made the perfectly outrageous claim that you need to be saved or baptized through their ministry in order to be justified in God's sight. That is doctrinal error, since salvation is not through church membership but through relationship to Jesus Christ.

Victims of such error might not have questioned these assertions in the past because they never had another church experience to compare it to. Determining doctrinal error is not easy. Who, other than the Lord Jesus, is doctrinally pure? However, we are responsible before God to conduct ourselves in a manner that pleases him, and our doctrinal stand will affect how well we do that.

Approach the leadership with doctrinal concerns. Ask questions and anticipate answers with several Bible references. Don't accept obscure explanations based on a preeminent author or minister as confirmation from God that certain church teachings or practices are correct. Dig into your Bible—it cost many people their lives to get it to you—and know what you believe and why.

Since we are in the body of Christ, don't be afraid to step outside the borders of your church or denominational orientation to get answers. I am not a Baptist, but I wouldn't hesitate to read Baptist publications or talk with Baptist ministers about foundational Christian doctrines. If someone of another church background is truly born-again, they have the capacity to be used by our heavenly Father to minister to our spiritual needs. God has made us incomplete. We need these other brothers and sisters in Christ to help us discern both God's Word and His ways.

Probing questions to ask might be:

—Are you uncertain of some of the major doctrines your church espouses? Can they be proven biblically?

—Is there any evidence of exclusivity? In other words, does your church claim to have cornered the market on certain biblical truths such as water baptism, eschatology, or spiritual gifts?

—Does your church welcome cross-pollination with other churches or ministries? Do you read literature from other Christian sources? If not, why not?

When diagnosing your church's spiritual health, a sixth issue we need to deal with is *how it addresses major problems.* Does the leadership in your church face them squarely, or do they, in effect, put bandages on them? Moral failure in today's church is very prevalent among leaders. When this is the case, the standards of I Timothy 3:1-7 must be met. That leader is not disqualified from serving in leadership capacity. Restoring the spiritual life of that leader with this family must be the priority for this life with the help of other leaders close to the situation. In today's church, however, because we seem so concerned to get that talented leader back in the pulpit, some churches disregard Scripture, apply a type of bandage to the problem, and then are surprised when the same problem in larger form appears months or years later.

The Scriptures do not demand that a fallen leader be restored to his office as if that were God's major purpose for his life. In many instances, God could care less about his titular role in the church. His focus, as always, is that leader's present relationship with him. We attach more importance on his role as pastor/leader than the Scriptures do. Every member of the body of Christ is important and has a part to play. The way most Christians seem to think today, Jesus is the head, the pastor is the upper half of the body, and the rest of the members are insignificant additions.

In reality, the average church member is no less important to the church than the pastor, biblically speaking. God appoints and anoints leadership. Pastors are vital to the direction of the local assembly, but so are deacons and individual members who use their callings to bless the church. Seminaries, Bible schools, Christian television, and periodicals have been instrumental in creating an unhealthy picture of what a pastor is supposed to be. When a leader is faced with the reality of stepping down from his office because of Scripture violations, he might feel as though he would like to die. Why? Because the image of pastor in his mind is often one built out of the concept of being indispensable to the furtherance of his own church. A careful reading of the New Testament reveals that no office is designed to be of more importance to God than another. Each has a specific function, but the individual members are of equal importance.

Church boards need to examine provisions for occasions when leaders fail, so that they can find the assistance they need to repair personal problems. Returning to ministry should be a back-burner item, and considered only if other leaders are satisfied that those criteria that best express their church's beliefs and mission have been met.

Questions that are important include:

—Is the pastor married to his spouse or to the church? In other words, is he allowed to have a family life complete with rest and relaxation, or do church needs consume his time?

—What sort of resources are made available to the family life of the church? Are all sermons and/or seminars related to biblical doctrines at the expense of family needs? Is the leadership actively providing teaching, speakers, or video presentations that train members how to be better husbands, wives, or parents? If not, why?

—Is there a clear, written document that spells out how the church scripturally deals with fallen leadership? Is there an understood process for temporarily or permanently replacing the pastor due to the above circumstances or unforeseen things like sickness or death?

There is nothing so sacred about "the ministry" that we need to violate its standards to stay in it.

We have made the position of minister so overblown in its importance that man would feel totally humiliated and ashamed to simply admit he has a need. We do not place that kind of pressure on other Christians. There is no precedence to put that kind of pressure on a leader. He ought to have the sort of relationship with other leaders whereby he can step down in order to meet God's standards, knowing that he will have the full support of both his church and other leaders.

In considering the spiritual condition of your church, stop a moment and see yourself as a mirror reflection of the sort of fruit your church produces. How is your spiritual life? When I was under the influence of Good News Chapel, my relationship with Christ reached a plateau and stayed there for several years. God seemed a million miles away. The joy of salvation was seldom if ever experienced anymore. Prayer was a drudgery. Oftentimes days passed with the Bible remaining on the table unopened. My Christian walk went from being exhilarating to depressing. The zeal I first felt when I was a new Christian and the desire I had to see the gospel of Jesus Christ proclaimed was gone. I believed that many of the things we were doing as a fellowship were unethical, but I also believed that God would straighten out the leadership. Underneath this belief was the fear that if I challenged Mike's authority, I might be struck down by God's judgment.

Seemingly endless conflicts and controversies enveloped the leadership of our church, thwarting any real progress towards reaching the lost for Christ. We developed a "siege mentality," looking for and expecting outsiders to try to change or destroy us. I cannot honestly remember more than one three-day period when my gut was not tied up in knots over a whole gamut of unspiritual problems.

One such occasion may serve to illustrate this point. Jim Rice (not his real name) had served as an elder in the early days of Good News Chapel. Due to a number of factors, not the least of which was a former drug habit, Jim backslid, returning to a life of sin.

One day he showed up with the apparent aim of reforming our church. His method: close the ministry down and let everyone go his or her way with Jesus. There were other details that made his proposals nothing less than absurd. However, our reaction to him characterized the sort of siege mentality I have already mentioned.

Before our dealings with Jim were concluded over the next year, we had fought him on virtually every level—except prayer. Public arguments, threats, police action, court appearances, and—believe it or not—an actual fist-fight between Mike (now a sick man) and Jim took place for the purpose of ridding our church of this menace.

What began as a disagreement accelerated into a series of fiascoes. Our testimony as believers was muddied as we schemed to defeat this human foe. The final outcome was settled finally in court, but not before Mike was forcibly ejected by the judge for his habitual and angry outbursts.

By subjugating my conscience and doing what I knew inherently to be wrong, my spiritual integrity was compromised. My spiritual life was weak instead of strong. If being involved fully in your church is neutralizing instead of strengthening your faith, ask *why*? If this church is healthy, *why* aren't you growing? Is there unconfessed sin in your life, or is the church manifesting fruit that doesn't resemble Jesus Christ?

The Scriptures encourage us to "judge ourselves" (1 Cor. 11:13). Perhaps now is the right time to take stock of your own spiritual condition before God.

—Are you still in love with Jesus?

—Is your life characterized by spiritual joy, peace, and faith?

—How is your devotional life?

—Is it a joy to serve Christ in your church?

—Is your relationship with your leaders healthy? In other words, do you trust them?

—Are you continuing to grow spiritually? If not, have you examined your own life to see if this is due to any sin on your part?

—Have you asked a good friend to help you see whether there is "any wicked way" in you?

Removing the mote out of leadership's eyes can be difficult if a beam is in our own. In all fairness, we cannot blame any church or leader for our own spiritual failures.

Do you still invite people to church? I reached a point at Good News Chapel where I had no desire to evangelize. Deep down, I knew that our church was a poor example of Christianity. The thought of inviting friends, relatives, or acquaintances to church was inconceivable to me. I reasoned, "Why should they come to church and be as miserable as I am?" It would seem more a gesture of hate than love to bring people to a place where they would be subjected to rude treatment, unethical behavior, and dubious financial practices.

As Christians, we ought to be excited about the church to which we belong! What good is it to share the gospel with people if you are ashamed to bring them to your church? The Body of Christ is a powerful, living expression of God in this earth. If you cannot in good conscience recommend your own church, how can you confidently expect to obey the Great Commission of Matthew 28:19, ". . . Go and make disciples of all nations . . . teaching them to obey everything I have commanded you." If your church is perverting the commandments of Christ, you will be sending people into deception rather than seeing them liberated in Christ. Jesus said, "But if anyone causes one of these little ones who believe in me to sin, it would be better for him to have a large millstone hung around his neck and to be drowned in the depths of the sea" (Matt. 18:6). That doesn't sound to me like, "Well done, thou good and faithful servant!" Ask yourself: "Have I stopped inviting people to church? Do I feel the need to make excuses to people outside the church about leadership decisions and actions?"

So why are you staying? Perhaps because deep within many of us is the belief that our efforts to change the way things are done in the church may bring it back to its original beauty. At the risk of being redundant, when there is a proper channel of appeal and accountability, such a conviction may be valid.

However, if there is secret sin in leadership, the determination to keep things from being uncovered will stand in front of you like a brick wall.

Martin Luther spent much time and effort before and during the time of the Reformation attempting to rebuild the Catholic church from within. He failed. Multitudes of people have attempted to repair religious systems through the centuries with few visible changes in the way authoritarian leadership does business. Remaining committed to a problem church is based upon a central, yet false assumption: That God is interested in restoring it!

We are emotionally and historically tied to an organization. God is not motivated in that way. He cares not whether an institution survives or fails. His main concern is whether or not his Church is continuing to be built. His Church is not the organization called First Baptist, St. Mary's, or Good News Chapel. We often commit ourselves to restoring what was a good church organization to a place of health again. This is an honorable quest, but in the final analysis, it may not be God's interest.

It has been my experience that the Lord would rather see his children investing themselves in the work of preaching and living the gospel than in devoting their energies to fighting wicked leadership in order to see an organization once again run biblically. We need to consider just how valuable the organization is to God in the first place. If years are spent struggling with unrepentant or ungodly leadership over the control of any institution, how are the purposes of God being served?

When a person has thought about his own experience within the church, his relationship to the pastor and other leaders (as well as to church members), and the growth he has experienced through the years, it is not easy to just say, "Good-bye!" The temptation to commit ourselves even deeper to save the ship is strong. Inwardly we may feel that our motive to do so is godly—but is it? We may find that we are motivated by pride. It is not easy to admit that the church you have belonged to is no longer viable. These are just a few guidelines to consider. Church members are responsible to know what they believe and why they believe it. No church, regardless of size or influence in the community, is beneath rendering account to its members. Some churches seem to require that you check your brains at the door. They need to be challenged. God's Word does not exalt foolishness.

It might be a good time to assess what is really going on in your own church. We will all stand before God one day. Are you personally ready to answer for the decisions you are agreeing with by being a member of your church? We cannot afford the luxury of hiding our heads in the sand and waiting for things to get better. Problems left alone get worse. If you examine your options in the light of Judgment Day, you will be apt to put aside the fear of what men might say to be sure that your involvement in your church is pleasing to God.

Chapter 3

I QUIT!

So here I was, pastor of my own Good News Chapel Outreach Center, about an hour's drive from the main headquarters, leading a small congregation, and trying to suppress a gnawing question: Why was ministry so ineffective?

I had come to this new community with high hopes but soon discovered that few people seemed truly interested in the things of Christ. Of those I did get the opportunity to minister to, few seemed to be truly helped. There was no measurable change in their lives because of my input. The few who did become members kept returning for counseling for the same sinful habits. There appeared to be no power in the gospel I was preaching as the solution to those habits. I wondered what was wrong with my preaching, teaching, and leading, since no visible evidence of godly change was occurring in peoples' lives.

More troubling still, was the issue of physical healing. I came from a background that embraced the claim that the sick could be healed through the power of the Holy Spirit. I believed what the Scriptures taught on praying for sick people but did not have a track record of results. In fact, people I prayed for usually grew worse after I said, "Amen!" It got to a point where I hated to do hospital visitations, or be asked to fulfill the duty of James 5:14,15: "Is any one of you sick? He should call the elders of the church to pray over him and anoint him with oil in the name of the Lord. And the prayer offered in faith will make the sick person well; the Lord will raise him up. If he has sinned, he will be forgiven." I knew that the person would remain just as sick after I prayed as before.

Of course, I could console myself with the knowledge that the home church was exactly the same, but that brought no solace. I was hungry for the God of the Bible, and I knew that the community I was attempting to reach would not be moved by anything less.

If I was just experiencing a "dry" time in my Christian walk, it had been lasting awfully long. Christianity had become too mundane for me to stomach. Something was wrong . . . but what?

I owed a great deal to Mike and Good News Chapel. It was through this ministry that a seventeen-year-old boy had been transformed into a recognized minister of the Gospel of Jesus Christ. I learned a great deal about personal responsibility from this ministry. I had met my wife there and personally witnessed Mike's tears of joy as we stood before him in our wedding garments. How could I now question the teachings I had been raised on?

But Good News Chapel had also transformed recognized leaders into paranoid squealers. Instead of going to the pastor with a view to helping erring brothers be restored to faith in Christ, we went to Mike to "inform" on brothers who were not acting in perfect harmony with our unwritten and unbiblical policies. Good News had remolded people who possessed a burning desire to preach the gospel into people committed to shoveling cow flops into manure piles each and every Saturday of the year. The teacher in me screamed at the ludicrousness of the situation. How could I not question what was going on?

My older brother gave me a booklet during this time, which would eventually change my circumstances. It was written by an author well known for his teachings on the subject of faith. I had always detested him. Naturally, I had never actually read any of his literature, but Mike had spoken so disparagingly of him, he had to be a false teacher.

On one particularly depressing day, I read this little booklet. My intention in reading it was not to seek help but to systematically refute its "false doctrines." Imagine my surprise when this booklet instead refocused my attention on the authority of God's Word! The lights began to turn on inside. Though I had prided myself on being "Word-centered," my beliefs were in actuality built upon the teachings of men. Soon, I began to question everything I believed, searching the Scriptures for proof.

I wasn't ready to start visiting other churches or talking to other ministers, but in the privacy of my own home, I was making that visit through the pages of this little booklet by a nationally known speaker. And while I would never become a disciple of the author, my spirit was sufficiently challenged that God was still moving miraculously in the lives of men and women, in spite of what I had experienced over the last several years.

With renewed vision, I devoured the Scriptures and uncovered truths I had previously ignored. Through prayer, I realized that I had come to accept minor truths of Scripture as the cornerstones of Christian faith instead of major doctrines taught by the apostles. By building my pastorate upon the shaky foundations of man's ideas, I was ignoring the true foundation, which is Christ, and dooming my church to failure. THIS was the cause of the fruitlessness that had been plaguing me for so long!

I began to take risks, asking key questions of another elder in the church. Why did we ask people to prove their spirituality by investing time in church maintenance instead of committing themselves to their families? Where did the Bible authorize us to settle our conflicts with lower-level leaders by chewing them out? What about I Peter 5:4 warning not to lord it over others? As we spent time talking things over in various contexts, I could see that he too was troubled. The church's methods were not just "a little bit off base." They were wrong.

Yet, I still carried a sense of dread within me. I was afraid to bring these things up, fearing that God would turn his back on me if I challenged "his anointed."

A few months passed before the inevitable happened. During one of our monthly "forums," I found myself in open conflict with Mike.

The idea of a monthly forum was Mike's idea. He felt it would be good to designate one night per month when the congregation could ask and receive answers to questions they had about Christian living. These questions were answered by a panel made up of the church elders.

On this particular evening, Mike was noticeably discouraged. A good friend of his had written a book reversing nearly every position he had taken as a national Christian speaker. Exhausted by his illness, Mike was in no mood to field questions, and I wondered why he had chosen that night to join us.

Mike dominated the evening. No other elder had much to say, since virtually all the questions were answered by the pastor. What made matters particularly tricky, was that I personally disagreed with nearly everything he did say!

Mike's theology, on this bizarre occasion, became a curious and destructive blend of predestination, the sovereignty of God, and outright fatalism. To the less theological of my readers, Mike was informing the congregation that every event that happens to Christians is ordained of God.

One woman asked, "then why pray?" Her question was appropriate. Mike responded that we should pray because Jesus commanded us to. He seemed to be denying that God could ever be asked to intervene in the affairs of men, since He caused each event to occur to begin with. As successive questions were raised, Mike's answers became more and more contradictory . . . even challenging some of the biblical principles upon which the church was founded.

Seated with the other elders, facing the congregation, I fixed my gaze at a corner of the ceiling to the rear of the assembled members. The adrenaline began flowing as my heart pounded in my chest. I was faced with a dilemma: If Mike's statements were left unchallenged, I would demonstrate that I agreed with him and be denying what I believed the Bible taught. On the other hand, if I confronted him, World War III might take place in full view of all. Complicating this conflict, deep down, I knew that Mike's answers were more a result of discouragement than serious theological exposition on his part. I prayed fervently that this meeting would conclude without my saying a word.

Mike rose to leave, which had become the standard prelude to closing our meetings. I began to breathe easier, and then, almost at a whim, he addressed me. "What do you think, Case?" The silence was deafening. I was backed into an inescapable corner, and there was no way out but forward. I closed my Bible, and as gently as I knew how told him I could not agree with his statements. He was totally unprepared for that.

I then outlined what God had been teaching me over the last several months of intensive Bible study, especially in relation to God's ability to heal the sick. No, God had not always healed every sick person, but yes, we were always called upon to seek him for healing. I then cited a recent case in my own church of a man who had been instantaneously healed in response to the prayer of faith.

Mike expressed his doubts of such a modern-day miracle and demanded proof from doctors. Then, and only then, would a bona-fide miracle be accepted. (Both doctors who were involved with the case would not sign anything for fear of malpractice suits. However, one, a Jewish man, could offer no explanation for his patient's complete reversal. He told him that whatever he was doing, to keep doing it!)

The meeting seemed to end without much incident. It was not obvious at that time what would happen next. Mike and I talked semi-privately, and he did not appear upset. This was tough for him. After all, this was "little Mike" seeming to proclaim that he knew better than "big Mike" what God teaches in the Bible. He was mystified . . . and threatened. I began to get an uneasy feeling about what might happen soon.

Two days later, I was called to "come up to the farm," where I was asked to publicly rescind my statements. Accused of "not remembering where I came from," I found my integrity challenged with an erratic and shameful display of yelling, false accusation, and innuendo, which only served to reinforce the conviction in my spirit that I had done the right thing in the first place. Mike was quieted down by his wife yet continued to challenge my statements and make me feel isolated by insisting that I was the only church member who held such views— something I knew to be patently untrue. Nevertheless, not wanting to be the cause of a church split, I deferred to some of Mike's "suggestions," and the following week publicly apologized for the effect of my statements. This "apology," needless to say, left a lot of confusion in the minds of the church members who heard the reality of my announcement. I was apologizing to Mike, while remaining opposed to some of his convictions.

As a direct result, I was no longer trusted to address t¹ "mother" church. Whenever I was absent, I returned to l. that unflattering comments had been made about me—some times from the pulpit, sometimes in semi-private conferences with individuals. I remained estranged from Mike and though still functioning as a pastor, an outsider among the leadership team.

You would think that such events would have left me depressed and defeated. That is what I would have thought, too. But instead of feeling my convictions grow weaker as a result of this ostracism, they were instead growing stronger. These events gave me the opportunity to interact with an increasing number of people outside of our church. More lights were coming on.

I opened up all the internal closets where I had stored boxes of teaching, and began cleaning them out, striving to replace them with solidly based biblical truth. Prayers were being answered more often. Joy returned along with her twin sister, Faith. Though an outlaw in my home church, I had more hope and peace in Christ than I had experienced in years.

I would love to report to you that this transformation took place in a matter of weeks. Truthfully, it took three years. Had I been less entrenched in this organization, the process might have gone more quickly. The confrontation that caused my exile was a gift of God in disguise. Because I now had more time to search the scriptures and think through my decisions, the blind obedience to Good News Chapel which had directed so much of my life, was disappearing.

Fruit began showing up in my life and character. By digging through the Scriptures and applying its principles, I found an inner peace that puzzled Mike. Isolation had not led me to repent or left me spiritually high and dry. Instead, I was more joyful and excited about Jesus than I had been since the early days.

Mike made it difficult for me to remain in the church. One painful instance was when he decided that I would leave my pastorate to begin a new outreach. Though we had briefly discussed such a possibility, I was called into his office one day, and told to inform my congregation of four years that I would be leaving in three weeks! All pastoral responsibilities would be turned over to a man that many of the people did not even know.

Every fiber of my being screamed at me to resign and simply sever ties with Good New Chapel. At that time, God sent a person my way who counseled me to submit myself, and the Lord would prosper me. Reluctantly, I obeyed.

It is my opinion that Mike fully expected me to fail in this new venture. Instead, the new outreach flourished almost overnight. If I had chosen to leave the ministry, based on what I had seen with others, Mike would make it look like I was rebelling against his "biblical" authority. It would have appeared to all that the problem was me, instead of with the doctrines he was teaching.

In spite of these and other efforts to subvert my effectiveness at Good News, I remained. Years later, this perseverance for which I claim no credit, enabled Mike to welcome me back into his life as a friend. I believe that he finally realized I wasn't concerned with seizing power as much as with upholding Biblical truth. For eight months, we grew closer to each other and learned to respect each other's differences.

Then, one night, I received an emotional phone call from another member of the pastoral team. Pastor Mike had died of heart failure, a complication of his disease. I was numb with disbelief. For years his "near death" encounters at the local hospital had been followed by news that Mike had recovered. This time there was no warning. He was gone.

The funeral was well-attended—not only by church members, but by many who had left Good News Chapel years previously. Although Mike had failed us in a number of key areas, we still recognized that God had used him to touch our lives. Many others acknowledged that he had been a gifted minister. I mention this, since the impression I have been giving, is of a sinister, manipulative man who served Christ only for what he could gain. In simple fact, Mike was as much a victim of false teaching as we were. His life was more complex than I would ever be able to share in a book. There are events I could write about which would cast him in a better light. But please begin to understand. My purpose is not the exposing of Mike's faults to justify my own actions. My purpose in sharing these unflattering things about my former pastor is to allow his mistakes to stand out as a warning beacon to all leaders who think it could never happen to them.

Soon after Mike's death, our leadership team, now comprised of three pastors, embarked on the noble, yet difficult task of rebuilding the original vision of Good News Chapel. Together, we spent long hours pouring over difficult questions of why and how our church had gone off the beaten path as well as what should be done to fix it.

We attempted to restructure many of Good News Chapel's basic operations, being careful to coordinate with Mike's family who now had a vested interest in the ministry. Mike had left Christine as the undisputed head of the men's program, and had appointed his eldest son to the post of administrator for both the men's program and the church months before his death. The input of leadership was never sought in these appointments. To challenge Mike's right to appoint these family members was akin to attacking Mike's right to pastor. We did not like this arrangement (particularly with respect to his son who was not a spiritual man), but we dutifully kept our mouths closed at the time.

Our aim now was to more closely reflect biblical ideals and principles, rather than the human patterns of power and control that had been strangling the spiritual life of our fellowship over the last several years. To our surprise, we repeatedly hit walls of resistance from Mike's family.

Understandably, any change in the way the church ran was scary to Mike's family. There existed an allegiance to upholding every principle Mike had instituted—not because it was right—but because to do anything different was in some way defiling his memory.

Additionally, Mike had not really prepared his wife or children for his death. It became unclear just who was in charge of what portion of the church. Mike and his family had direct control over the men's program and its operation. Now that he had died, his wife assumed this position, but what part did she play in the spiritual leadership of the church overall? His son was the administrator. Just what did that mean? To him it meant managing the finances of all the churches. Yet his son did not make decisions based on Scripture or the counsel of godly men. While our advice was sought in some areas, it was ignored in others. Since Mike had little understanding of what it was to be accountable to anyone, his family was also poorly equipped to accept accountability as anything less than a threat.

Restoring the church to its original vision was now compounded by ridicule from his family. "That's not the way Mike (or, my father) would have done this" became a standard obstacle to change. Nearly each member of his immediate family took their turns interpreting what Mike would have wanted if he were still alive. We had no way of shifting their focus. The issue wasn't what Mike would have wanted, or even what we wanted. The issue was: How would the Lord Jesus want Good News Chapel to function?

This resistance continued for more than a year. First it was mild, then deliberate. The pastors had no influence over Mike's family or the men's program, which they continued to operate.

Finally, after seemingly countless meetings to discuss our alternatives, we agreed that God's leadership for our lives and the biblical course of action was simply to resign. We came to the conclusion that God had not called us to "fix" Good News Chapel but reconnect with the Body of Christ around us.

Mike's family seemed unconcerned. His son expressed the belief that our actions would have little effect upon the future of Good News Chapel.

Within weeks, without our saying a word to them, without our inviting them to join us or offering them anything, 90 percent of the membership followed us out the doors. We later learned that many of them had stayed with the church not out of loyalty to Mike's memory, but out of loyalty to us.

The word "cult" is a scary one. It immediately conjures up visions of Jim Jones and cyanide-laced Kool-Aid. Good News Chapel was not a cult, but it was cultic. It was a legitimate church in the New Testament sense, but its extremes encouraged allegiance more to church leadership than to the Lord.

Part of the process of starting over for me was to acknowledge that I had not only participated in a church with cult-like practices, I had been a leader. I had not only been oppressed, I had been an oppressor. My fear of Mike had been much of the basis for decisions I made. I was guided too often by what I thought Mike wanted, and too rarely by what the Bible teaches. Like it or not (and I didn't!), I had been a willing participant in the process by which Good News Chapel had adopted cult-like processes.

There is no sin in being cautious and nothing is wrong with waiting to make a decision until we are clear we have the facts. But caution becomes sin when we let our fear of a leader prevent us from responding to facts by taking courses of action outlined in the Scriptures. As a part of the leadership team, I had done wrong and perpetuated wrongdoing by continuing in leadership under ungodly conditions. We were wounded, weary, and uncertain of the future. How could we lead this people who had been bold enough to follow us out? Where were we going?

Chapter 4

THE QUESTION ISN'T WHETHER TO LEAVE—BUT HOW?

Wherever you may be in our world, you will find churches in various stages of growth or decay. The difficulty with books like this is that people might use them as an excuse to exit a church for personal instead of biblical reasons. Every church has problems! A brief reading of the New Testament will demonstrate a myriad of people-problems, which each congregation faced. The church in Corinth, for example, was heading the wrong way in a number of areas: its focus on various preachers instead of God; its members' lack of loving concern for each other; its disorderly and disrupted worship services and its severe lack of proper moral standards, among many other things. Paul addressed these errors, and the subsequent changes the Corinthians made demonstrate how successful Paul was in his admonitions.

Jesus spoke directly to seven churches through John in the book of Revelation. Most of these churches had problems that He required them to fix. Churches do make mistakes, and certain allowances have to be made for this. The last thing we need today is a group of roving church connoisseurs, who go from place to place "tasting" how delectable area churches are to see whether or not they will join. As long as humans belong to churches, there will be problems, which can only be solved by God's wisdom. The key test whether a church simply has problems or is a problem church is whether leadership is willing to listen and respond to correction. In Corinth, the leadership responded to Paul's rebukes and took steps to correct both the moral failures and the doctrinal errors being allowed in the church. The depth of their repentance is recorded for us in II Corinthians 7:11. Prior to Paul's rebuke, this church was a soul-winning mega-church with terrible problems. Responding through repentance changed them from a problem church (one under God's judgment) to a church with problems (one under God's grace).

All of us, including leaders, are imperfect beings needing the grace of God daily. We have all done things as Christians for which we are ashamed. Making mistakes is not an issue with God, but responding to his correction is. When we consider this question in light of deciding whether or not to leave our church, it might be better to update a question we should have asked ourselves when we first became members: "Is there anything about this church that makes me believe that God wants me to stay here?" Is there now clear evidence of doctrinal error? Have you approached leadership with your concerns if this is so? What was the response? Was the problem resolved? How?

People leave churches everyday. Four primary reasons are: rebellion; satanic deception; social or relational problems; and frustration with apparently irreparable situations. Nothing is worse than rebellion against God, but as we have mentioned, some church leaders use this term against anyone who doesn't agree with them. Rebellion is the unwillingness of an individual to submit to God's rule. We live in a lawless era, and discipline remains at an all-time low. The claims of Christ as Lord of our lives are very threatening—especially because He intends to be Lord of our lives! There are believers in Christ who find the Christian life more of a commitment than they bargained for, and so they leave a church because they are being convicted by the Holy Spirit, and they don't like it.

Jesus addressed this issue when he told his disciples to count the cost (Luke 14:28). Christ has paid the price for our sins, but we must bear the cost of serving Him. We will suffer persecution (2 Tim. 3:12). We will know tribulation (John 14:1). We will know suffering (Phil. 1:29). There are some who hear the gospel, but like seed on stony ground dismiss themselves from the church when they are rejected by the world for their Christian testimony (Mark 4:17).

Secondly, people leave churches because of satanic deception. In other words, they do not resist the devil. A key satanic strategy has always been to isolate Christians from the local church. Working in league with people's fears and weaknesses, Satan arranges circumstances and events in ways that distract followers of Christ from participating in the church. Other priorities enter in, and before long, the once-zealous heart of the believer grows cold. So there are those who leave, not as the result of deliberation and choice but through fear of others, forgetfulness, or the deceptive cares and riches of this life (Luke 8:12-14).

Thirdly, people leave churches due to various social and relational concerns. Perhaps they never sensed that they fit in, for example. We are complex human beings, each with a wide array of personal and spiritual needs. We require love and affirmation by our peers, as well as the Lord. When that longing is ignored, people come to believe that their contribution to a group of people is insignificant. Leaving that assembly is the next logical step. Because God has designed us to be social beings, friendship is one of the strong bonds that tie us to Christ's church. When people are unable for whatever reason to form deep friendships with other members, they will vacate the pews of a given church.

Becoming a part of others is vital to experience the fullness of Christianity in the local church. Some never let their guard down long enough to entrust themselves to the other members or to the leadership. They keep themselves from being hurt, but wind up hurting from loneliness anyway.

Many of these relational and social concerns usually accompany people with less of an investment in their particular church.

Finally, and more in line with our discussion to this point, people leave their church because it has become so "unfixable" that no other option makes sense. We are not talking here about the casual churchgoer. We are referring to those who have invested their lives into their local church; people who have prayed for and labored with other church members to reach the community for the good of the kingdom of God. After making such an extended commitment, how do you know if God wants you to leave the institution to which you have given your life ? Is there a way to discern the difference between a church that is cultic and a church that can be fixed?

Matthew 18:15-20 describes an important process set up by the Lord Jesus to settle disputes in the congregation. When a church acts on principles, its members will operate with one heart and one mind.

> If your brother sins against you, go and show him his fault, just between the two of you. If he listens to you, you have won your brother over.
> But if he will not listen, take one or two others along, so that every matter may be established by the testimony of two or three witnesses.
> If he refuses to listen to them, tell it to the church; and if he refuses to listen even to the church, treat him as you would a pagan or a tax collector.
> I tell you the truth, whatever you bind on earth will be bound in heaven.
> Again, I tell you that if two of you on earth agree about anything you ask for, it will be done for you by my father in heaven,
> For where two or three come together in my name, there am I with them.

Handbook of Church Discipline, by Jay Adams, lays out important truths to consider when bringing correction to other members of the body of Christ. Here is a sampling of his observations:

> • Discipline . . . is God's provision for good order in His church that creates conditions for the instruction and growth of the members. Discipline has a positive function.

• God is honored by church discipline, rightly adminis-
tered, and is greatly dishonored by its absence.

• . . . Leadership exists to build up the members in their
faith and to help them discover, develop, and deploy
their gifts for mutual ministry among themselves.

Adams asserts that there are five steps directly mentioned
or alluded to in the Matthew 18:15-18 process. They are *self-
discipline*, in which a person recognized that he or she has
strayed from God's commands and exercises self-control in
coming back to God. This is the most fundamental discipline in
which no other person is involved. An individual is simply
convicted by the Holy Spirit through reading the Scriptures or
by the expounding of God's Word and then responds by correcting his own behavior.

The second step is *one–on–one*. Adams points out that "The
principle followed in Matthew 18:15, is that a matter must be
kept as narrow as the event itself. . . . Whenever an unreconciled
condition exists between two believers, there is no option left:
discipline must be pursued." The aim for a one–on–one meeting is to bring about reconciliation between the parties. The
offended party goes privately to the alleged offender and "tentatively" rebukes him. I say tentatively, because the offended
party must leave room for explanation. There might be an
offense based on misunderstanding rather than wrongdoing.

The third step, should the previous two fail, is *one or two
others*. When does this step become operational? Adams states:
"In Matthew 18:16 the operative phrase is 'if he won't listen to
you.' At each stage, what moves the process ahead a step is the
refusal of the offender to be reconciled." In this stage, witnesses
are brought in who ". . . attest to and confirm . . . every word."
Adams goes on to say that these witnesses act not only as such,
but as counselors as well. If they discover that there is no
misunderstanding, but that an actual offense has been committed, ". . . they should proceed to ascertain all the facts, evaluate
these according to biblical standards, state the issues in biblical
terms, and suggest a plan for solving the problem based on
biblical principles."

In the first three steps, the church discipline being exercised is informal in nature. It has remained a relatively private matter. In step four, the offense/sin becomes formal should the offender refuse to listen. This step is called, *"telling it to the Church . . ."*

Adams points out that doing this is not simply standing up in the midst of a church service and blurting out the offense committed. In the interest of good order, he recommends that the first stage of telling it to the church is done by informing the elders. The elders are then free to investigate the matter and may properly arrange to call a meeting for baptized membership. The unsaved and those who are visitors should not be included in this event.

Finally, Adams brings us to stage five, which he calls *"removal from the midst."* As this step implies, the offender is told to leave the church and is unwelcome until such time as repentance is sought. (Adams mentions a number of practical suggestions for churches to follow in this procedure, which are helpful, but not pertinent to our focus here.) Contrary to what many Christians might think, removing from the midst is still one of the most loving things God does for an erring member. It was through such a process that repentance was obtained in the life of a fornicator mentioned in I Corinthians 5.

Adams' observations and conclusions are extremely helpful in formulating an approach to bringing correction to a church leader. Matthew 18:15-20 does not differentiate between clergy and laity. Neither does God! Leaders are therefore not exempt from being approached. This is Jesus' method for dealing with offenses and sin.

It is also important to note that after properly resolving disputes according to the steps outlined by Christ, answered prayer will result. We seldom consider our relationships with other members of the body of Christ when we approach God in prayer. However, Jesus made it clear on several occasions that unresolved issues between church members hinder his power from moving on their behalf.

Matthew 18:15-20 governs relationships in which there has been an offense. Some do not leave churches because they have been personally offended by what has been said or done. They simply find that the preaching, teaching, and example of leadership do not line up to what they believe to be New Testament standards. Such people, in my opinion, should communicate their feelings to leaders well before the need to leave becomes crucial. However, if the leadership demonstrates no willingness to change, it is not necessary to confront leadership to leave a church that has gone bad. We are each accountable for our Christian walk and those God has entrusted to us. Christ has not called us to subject ourselves to what is not of him (Mark 4:24).

For those who have taken offense at things the leadership has said or done, or those who have participated in the leadership process, it is imperative that leaving be accomplished with a clear conscience. Biblical principles of appealing to authority in an attitude of humility before God ought to be the road we take if exemplifying Jesus is our goal.

When offended personally, there is a danger of staining ourselves with sin in trying to deal with the offense. A good friend of mine who struggled with the ungodly behavior of church leadership within his own church remarked to me, "I jumped in the sewer in order to rescue my church, and got dirty myself." Satan would love to turn spiritual warfare into a battle of fleshly arguing between Christian leaders if he can. We need to speak the truth in love, but we must display Christlike character in doing so, or we will become as filthy as the sin we are trying to clean up.

Don't misunderstand what I am trying to say. Addressing sin is not likely to bring praise from leaders who are determined to hide it. However, Christians ought to be able to point to and use an orderly step-by-step procedure that closely resembles the principles of Matthew 18:15-18.

A man I'll call Sam attended Grace Bible Church for several years. Early on his faithfulness was recognized, and he was appointed to serve as a deacon in the church. He zealously served Christ and was fully supportive of the goals and directions the church as a whole was taking.

As time went on, he and others became increasingly alarmed at decisions being made by the pastor. Many of these decisions appeared to be arbitrary and self-exalting. Public and private instances strongly indicated that the elders who served with the pastor were little more than "yes men," always defending the actions of the pastor whether they had the facts of any given situation or not. Added to this were testimonies of former members, whose verifiable accounts of mistreatment caused Sam to reflect a great deal as to his future with the church. Over a period of several months, Sam made appointments with a variety of current and former church members, asking them many questions.

There were also ethical issues that needed resolution. Sam talked to leadership about his concerns, but no action was taken. Through many such encounters, he finally decided to become a part of a group whose sole purpose was to address these same issues.

For many weeks, Sam met with members who had a long list of grievances against the leadership in general and the pastor in particular. Sam's contribution was to help separate fact from fiction. It was amazing how much "information" was based on slander and unconfirmed accounts. However, this group reached a point when they had sufficient evidence of wrongdoing to discuss it with the leadership of the church.

Sam, as spokesman of the group, called the pastor for a meeting to discuss these problems. Before this meeting, Sam phoned me to inform me of his intentions. He believed that God was leading him not to simply address problems, but to offer scriptural solutions as well. Just before hanging up, Sam remarked, "When this is all said and done, if my wife and I leave Grace Bible Church, we will still see the pastor and church leadership at the supermarket."

In effectively administering church discipline, we need to realize that unless we move out of town, the people we have confronted will not simply vanish from our lives. It is imperative before God and man that we be able to face those we have confronted anywhere with a clear conscience, knowing that we acted scripturally in our facts, attitudes, and methods.

In Sam's case, he and several others presented their evidences to the pastor in the presence of the elders. The elders chose to defend the pastor, making it clear that their only purpose for hearing the accusations was to bring correction to Sam and the men with him. There was no resolution, and the team disbanded. With nowhere else to appeal, they chose as individuals to leave Grace Bible Church and join other local ministries. Discipline was then left in God's hands, since all methods of appeal were exhausted. Sam departed without bitterness or resentment. He did not love the pastor less, nor did he take part in a slander campaign.

Months later, Sam's former pastor began to attempt change in his personal life and ministry. Only time will tell if the gentle-spirited team confrontation was used by God as part of His process of bringing about lasting repentance and change.

When you confront possible cultic leadership, following the Matthew 18 process, you find you are dealing not only with a person, but with a spiritual personality as well. I have known of cases where the leader's persona almost had the effect of casting a spell upon those who were determined to properly confront him. Many have reported that when they tried to talk with their pastor face–to–face, they wound up confused and intimidated without ever touching the real issues. Those who have encountered this type of situation have felt that they were not just confronting an individual, but a spiritual principality (Eph. 6:12). Satan does have an interest in keeping leadership deceived. By following these steps, you present a threat to his authority, which does not go unchallenged.

I know of two churches where sin was blatant, but the majority of the congregation felt perfectly comfortable in allowing the pastor to continue ministering without missing a beat. The leadership had actively participated in sexual immorality, yet people were unconcerned. In my experience, only a demonic entity can accomplish this kind of wholesale deception over an entire church. Christians who commit themselves to biblical confrontation need to prepare themselves for war . . . but not against flesh and blood. Ephesians 6:12-18 tells us how to "suit up" for such a battle.

Effective spiritual warfare comes through keeping in constant contact with our Commander and obeying His orders. The pattern I see Him use time and time again calls for us to apply scriptural principles and then to leave, if there is no evidence of repentance.

It is important to remember that God's objective may not be to rescue a church, but to judge it. We need to be sensitive to simply accomplishing what God intends us to do through the Scripture and prayer. I can think of several occasions when godly people have confronted leaders and been forced to leave a church, only to see that church fold within a short time, or else be rendered ineffective in the community. The judgment of each case must be left entirely up to God. We have our responsibility, and He has His. If we intrude into His business by trying to use carnal means to damage reputations, we will dirty ourselves in the process, and we will be judged by God, along with the leader we are trying to expose.

In all probability, your efforts to bring viable accountability to the leadership of a cultic church will go unappreciated. It is probable that your reputation will suffer considerably as questions are raised about your integrity. Satan will use other Christians loyal to the church to malign you and your family because they misunderstand your actions. Painful experiences like this are often part of the price you must pay to serve Christ. Peter said it this way: ". . . if you suffer for doing good and you endure it, this is commendable before God" (1 Pet. 2:20 b).

If the pastor's words or actions have offended you, and you have exhausted scriptural appeals, you must inform the church and walk away. Jesus does not tell us how to do this, though I believe that the method Jay Adams recommends is a good one. The end result is to provide other church members with both the necessary information and the steps taken to bring about reconciliation. Speaking from personal experience, *document everything*. When issues are left unresolved, the door is open for misinformation. The power of the pastorate affords the opportunity to spread slander with an air of legitimacy and respectability. It would be enormously helpful for you to have in your possession a written record of the events that took place, the people present, what was said and to whom, and so on, etc., for reference. If you are unclear about these things, your ability to help others is limited.

Some of you may be bothered by the prospect of "walking away." Deep down we all enjoy winning battles in a way that gains recognition. Your ego may suffer in this process of approaching a leader. If winning a power struggle against a manipulative leader is your objective, you have no right to claim to be a disciple of the Lord Jesus. The goal is to honor God by our adherence to His Word, demonstrating a spirit of reconciliation wherever possible. We are not responsible to see to it that a leader's reputation is destroyed.

In Matthew 5:22, Jesus warns us against calling another brother a "fool." The Greek word is *moros*, and denotes destroying the reputation of another. He condemned this as the worst form of anger, subject to the greatest punishment. In the verses that follow (23-26), Christ makes it clear that our objectives must be redemptive, for repentance is possible as long as they live.

Paul left us a clue as to how to deal with brothers who reject us and will not listen to godly counsel. Warning a fellow pastor, he says: "Alexander the metalworker did me a great deal of harm. The Lord will repay him for what he has done" (2 Tim. 4:14). The task of vengeance for wrongdoing belongs to God exclusively. He will right the wrongs, for he is the great equalizer.

If you must walk away, do so as cleanly as possible. Say what you need to say and depart, praying for the repentance of former leaders. In my case, we left as a team. All Matthew 18:15-18 processes were thoroughly exhausted as much as God, by his grace, permitted us to understand. God spoke clearly to our leadership that we were to leave and say absolutely nothing.

When we resigned, one of our pastors made it clear that we could no longer walk in agreement with the goals and purposes of Good News Chapel. He made it clear that ill will was not our motive in departing. At that meeting, there was no arguing or confrontation. Over the next several months, we bit down hard on our tongues, attempting to follow God's prime directive. It was painful to be silent and not to justify ourselves. God knew all along that this restriction would turn to our good.

The more you talk, the more you open yourself up to sinning with your words. Once you've made your decision, you need to leave judgment to God. Ours is not to justify our actions, but to serve our Lord.

Chapter 5

OUT OF CONTROL

You're out. The break has been made. You are no longer part of your former church. You hoped that leaving would solve so many problems, and that your new-found freedom would be close to heaven on earth—but it isn't. What happened?

Unless you have experienced it, no one can know the inner turmoil of leaving a church you once loved. You are angry at the way the church has gone sour—perhaps angry at leaders you once respected. Now you are left to sort out what was good from what was bad.

Emotionally, you are drained. Days and weeks of depression, guilt, and fear are nearly overwhelming. Harassment from within and without make you wonder whether you made the right decision—yet, you know you did.

If you are experiencing any of these emotions, you can be reasonably certain that you are normal, and that your present circumstances are temporary. None of us really knows the impact of breaking a relationship with a church until we actually experience it. It is painful and stressful.

At the same time you are sorting out what you believe, you find yourself mistrusting everyone—including yourself! You may reason, "My pastor failed me—who is to say any other pastor will not do the same?" It is normal to be overly suspicious of other leaders. Your trust in someone or an organization has been violated. In a very real way, it is like being spiritually raped, and the rapist acknowledges no guilt. Yet, an actual rape victim who chooses to live the experience over and over in her mind for the rest of her life will become emotionally crippled and unable to cope with the present.

Like the rape victim, it is not so easy to just dust yourself off and be on your way. You have been abused and violated. However, you cannot afford to live the rest of your spiritual life embittered against the leader who did it. You must forgive him. Unforgiveness binds *you*; it does not bind the object of the anger. And, God will hold you guilty, no matter how justified you might feel. Remember, unless you leave town, you will see these people over and over again. You need to be free of all hurt, bitterness, and anger. Jesus said, "Forgive them, they don't know what they do!" Can we afford to do less?

In the world in which we live, a person who has been raped must accept the awful reality that it happened, or risk bringing the anger of those feelings into all future relationships. Furthermore, she is required to allow the process of law to declare the offender either guilty or innocent. She cannot take the law into her own hands and carry out revenge without consequences.

A person who has been victimized by a spiritual leader must forgive that individual, and allow God to direct what steps to take or not to take. "It is mine to avenge; I will repay, says the Lord" (Rom. 12:19). Don't "jump in the sewer" attempting to do what is essentially God's task.

The Old Testament records an example for us to help solidify this principle. We read in I Samuel how David, then an outlaw in King Saul's eyes, went out of his way to do good for a man called Nabal. In the process of time, David asked a small favor of Nabal, whose negative reply was rude at best. In his anger, David purposed to treat Nabal like any other enemy of Israel by destroying him and his family.

Through the intercession of Abigail, Nabal's wife, David's anger was appeased. He released his anger and indignation to the Lord, and Abigail returned home. Not long after, following a night of drunkenness, she informed Nabal that she had spoken to David. When she did,

> . . . his heart failed him and he became like a stone.
> About ten days later, the Lord struck Nabal, and he died.
>
> When David heard that Nabal was dead, he said, "Praise be to the Lord, who has upheld my cause against Nabal for treating me with contempt. He has kept his servant from doing wrong and has brought Nabal's wrongdoing down on his own head."
>
> Then David sent word to Abigail, asking her to become his wife. (1 Sam. 25:37-39)

When we leave vengeance to God, we trust him to carry out His justice. It may be that our willingness to bless those who have harmed us will lead the victimizer to repentance, as in the case of Paul the apostle who watched his victim, Stephen, die, prior to his own conversion.

In other cases, God may choose to bring judgment upon those who do not respect the body of Christ (1 Cor. 11:30). There are not a few leaders who have died prematurely because they intentionally or through ignorance placed unnecessary and painful burdens upon other members of their church.

In either case, we make it difficult for God to work when we hold on to hatred or ill will, for to judge the victimizer, he who is just will have to judge us as well.

Leaving a church brings changes. One noticeable change for my wife and me when we left Good News Chapel was our schedule. All at once, we had time on our hands. Formerly, several nights per week plus all day Saturday were consumed with church-related activities. Now there were none.

Though this may seem strange, we actually developed guilt feelings for having this extra time. We had been subtly indoctrinated to believe that living our life apart from the church's programs and goals was somehow ungodly. Thinking back, we could see how much both of us had neglected our family so that the church's property was properly maintained. Many members had forced their families to be home alone several nights per week so that ineffective church programs could operate smoothly.

Through this type of thinking, we had come to believe that denying the legitimate needs of our family was somehow spiritual. I, for one, had great difficulty feeling right about placing my wife and children above the needs of the church. The fear of loving my family more than Christ kept me from enjoying them as God intended. For those trapped in cultic churches, God and the church itself have become inseparably entwined: To neglect ministry needs is to neglect God's will. In leaving, I needed to jettison a great deal of teaching and guilt, while holding on to biblical truth.

It had become second nature to fill our time with church activities. What do you do now that those activities have ceased? It may seem elementary, but you would be surprised how many hours I spent looking at the ceiling and being unable to make the smallest decisions. A large part of me was drawn to any activity that would help me dull the hurt inside. Television with its brainless approach to existence became my fleshly way of escaping for a short time.

In the same way, Jehovah's Witnesses, who leave the Watchtower, face many of the same things those who leave cultic churches face. They have been programmed to believe that all other churches are governed by Satan. As a result, you can imagine the suspicion and mental anguish each person experiences being thrust upon the entire church world. Whom do you trust? Which church is right? and so on.

A common experience for the ex-Jehovah's Witness is to go on a "binge" as a means of dealing with his frustration. That is, he throws off all restraint and begins smoking, swearing, drinking, and living immorally. Frustration often drives him to turn away from God altogether. Christians are different since we were not part of a false religion. Still, there is the same tendency in every one of us to become suspicious of other pastors or churches, and in frustration, despair of God altogether. Bitterness toward our former church can drive us toward making wrong decisions.

In the scheme of things, Satan sees us coming. He would like nothing better than to help our faith become shipwrecked. Our predicament is his opportunity to discourage us from ever being fruitful for the Lord again. Healing is what we need. Now is when we need it!

As former church members, we must rethink our values and decide what decisions have been made out of the wrong motivations. I discovered that many of the reasons I did things at Good News was the fear of making leaders angry, or from guilt that I wasn't doing enough for God's kingdom. My wife had struggled for quite some time with feelings of inadequacy, because as a result of her God-given maternal instincts, much of her time was consumed with raising children. False values instilled in her through the years had made her believe that if she wasn't heavily involved and supportive of the church's priorities, she was somehow out of God's perfect will.

Now, our decisions needed to be motivated out of obedience to God. Sometimes, obedience is simply listening, as is illustrated in the story of Martha and Mary. Martha was anxious with "busywork" for Jesus. Mary was seated quietly at his feet. Jesus commended Mary, but he gently rebuked Martha as someone who had chosen the less spiritual path. Most of us coming out of cultic churches might have felt inwardly as Martha did—that Mary was a lazy good-for-nothing. Jesus identified her as the more spiritual of the two women. We need to reassess what we are doing with our time and judge our actions in light of the Word of God and eternity. As one sister in Christ once said to me, "We are human beings not human doings."

A common tendency for those of us leaving cultic churches is to "throw out the baby with the bath water." That is, to be rid of everything—good and bad. This tendency is born out of total frustration with the idea of having to begin again after so long a time as a Christian. It is important to realize that not all of what we learned was evil. We need to reexamine Scripture, strengthening right beliefs and rejecting unbiblical teachings we received, which were not solidly based in God's Word.

Part of the inner turmoil we might also experience is the "love-hate" relationship we have with former leaders. On the one hand, we seem to despise what they have become. On the other, we remember what they once were and begin to make excuses for why they did what they did.

At Good News Chapel, Mike became terminally ill and remained in this condition for several years. He often experienced extreme pain and at times needed to be heavily medicated. Upon leaving Good News Chapel, we leaders would often discuss the decisions he had made, which had hurt either the church or his own family. During the same conversations, we would also discuss the sense of pity we felt toward him for the things he suffered. On the one hand, we held him responsible for actions he had taken. On the other, we excused him because of the tremendous physical pain he suffered.

In another church I know, the pastor had grown up in an atmosphere of parental rejection. Though the parishioners who left his church were angry at many of the ways in which they had been manipulated, nevertheless they continued to feel sorry for the things that the pastor suffered while growing up!

These sorts of mixed feelings toward a former leader help to create a great deal of inner emotional tension. "I know that there were things wrong, but was I right to leave?" some people will think. When I left, I tried not to despise what Mike had done. I struggled to remember the good times. What I found, however, is that even the faintest inquiry by another Christian about Good News Chapel would jump start my mouth into a thirty-minute dissertation on what led to its demise and why I left.

One solution, which is more productive than leaving the motor running on your tongue, is to follow what the Scriptures teach—and to pray for the one who abused you. Of course, in my case, he was already gone, but his family needed—and still needs—prayer. God wants us to leave the correction of the leader in his capable hands and pray for them, if all other avenues have been exhausted. It is insecurity that makes us feel as though we have to perfectly sort out where a leader went wrong. Only God truly knows, and our continuing responsibility is to lift that former leader up in prayer whenever we are tempted towards bitterness. Anger binds the one who has it.

While it is not always possible, this might be a good time to plan time away from your geographical location. Family members experience tremendous stress upon leaving a church. This can translate into more strained relationships between husband and wife or parents and children. There is much to think about, pray about, and act upon. However, you might not be equipped to handle it all at this time. Give yourself some room. It will take plenty of time to reformulate what your relationship to Christ is really supposed to be.

It is also quite healthy, wherever possible, to connect with other growing churches in your area. Attending seminars, going to a variety of different churches, talking to several church leaders, and examining the literature of other congregations all will help you get a feel for what is truly happening in the Body of Christ. Remember, much of the trouble began when we thought that our former church had all the answers. As a by-product of this thinking, we unknowingly cut ourselves off from what Jesus was doing around the corner from us. Guess what? There is a lot of catching up to do.

It is almost as if you have been away from your hometown for years. Upon returning, you find that there are lots of new people in the neighborhood. Landmarks you remember are gone, and old familiar places have been changed. In the same way, you have become isolated from what Christ has been doing in the larger body of Christ. It is time to find out about what the Holy Spirit has been doing while you've been away.

It is humbling to go to other churches and see that God has been moving there for some time. Like other churches I've mentioned, at Good News Chapel, we viewed ourselves in such a superior light that it was difficult to see why people went to other churches at all! This proud attitude needed to be broken in my life.

Leaving a cultic church after following scriptural steps is the first step back into reality. The second step is humbling yourself to accept other churches as being equal partners in the work of God. One church I am familiar with had the nicest building, the largest congregation, the finest children's outreach, and the best choir. Members were very smug about the superior revelations and tremendous programs this church seemed to have. When a severe lack of accountability in the pastor became apparent, members left en masse and were then confronted with the pride that had made them feel so smug years earlier. Few were prepared to deal with this pride and found going to other born-again churches in the region very taxing. None of these other churches, from a structural standpoint, could compare with their former assembly. It is true that the road out of error is the path of humility. Unless you plan to choose that path, you cannot be truly healed.

A good friend of mine who is a former Jehovah's Witness elder's wife told me of the persecution she and her husband experienced upon leaving that group. Old acquaintances made such terrible remarks about their character. As I conversed with her, she stated that it was good for them to experience such persecution. When I inquired as to why, she told me that they had been so "cocky" that they needed to be humbled by God in this way.

For those of us who have been a part of a church that went bad and stayed anyway, there are reasons why we stayed, which have little to do with doctrine or a certain point of view. The need for self-esteem and the weakening effect of other behavioral voids attract people to cultic churches and personalities. These needs and weaknesses must be dealt with properly.

Remember, God's objective is not simply to see you physically leave a bad church. His objective is to break within you the tendency to become wrapped up in the same system time after time. Satan's goal within the whole process is to destroy you. His desire is to maneuver your thoughts and emotions to a place where you believe, after coming through an awful experience, that the church of Christ is a waste of your time and commitment. He attempts to do this to divert us from the only place where we are likely to get the spiritual help we need: the church.

Chapter 6

I'VE LEFT THE CHURCH, BUT THE CHURCH DIDN'T LEAVE ME!

Wouldn't it be great if you could just join another church and start all over again with all your bad memories erased? You can't, you know. You have been infected, and like most infected people, you may be contagious!

How badly you are infected depends to a large degree on how long your church had been dysfunctional and how close you were to the center of the decision-making apparatus.

As mentioned earlier, when I left Good News Chapel, I did so with two other pastors. The three of us embarked on a journey to rediscover our true calling in Christ. We had spent many years of our Christian lives performing fruitless service to a church organization that had lost its direction. Now, we needed to be about the business of re-connecting with a more biblical model of Christianity.

Because we were all located in different cities many miles from each other, it became natural for us to refocus our ministerial attention upon the small congregations we pastored individually. My vision was no longer directed towards being part of a central organization but instead being the leader of a small church.

During this time of personal reconstruction, I would often think to myself how great it was to be free! Spiritually speaking, I felt as if I had left Egypt and passed through the Red Sea. Jesus was so fresh, new, and alive—it was like being born again, *again*! I so fully enjoyed this new-found freedom. I cannot begin to tell you the renewed sense of vision I experienced over simple things like offerings. To know that the money collected would actually be spent on things pertinent to my own congregation was like heaven to me!

Hungry to rejoin the body of Christ, I began introducing changes in our local congregation designed to dismantle many of our ineffective programs and put us back on track toward impacting the society in which we lived. Since I no longer spent the majority of my time serving the interests of an organization, I fully expected that my efforts would yield long-awaited results.

Still, like any ministry, we had our problems, and some of them frustrated me. Over the next several months, these frustrations escalated into daily tension. I grew more and more perplexed. Why weren't these problems being quickly and easily solved? From my vantage point, the cause of nearly all of my church's difficulties had been removed. Unconsciously, I now expected our local church to leap forward in unprecedented church growth and health.

After approximately one year passed, I chanced to attend a seminar for ministers. It was at this meeting that the Holy Spirit met me in a wonderful way. It was not by any words spoken by any of the speakers from the pulpit, since none of the topics addressed my particular need, yet God revealed to my inner man what was holding me back. *Even though I had left Good News, Good News had not left me!* Had I not been sure it was an impression from the Holy Spirit, I would have denied such a thought vehemently. But, God turned on the light by reminding me of a number of instances throughout the previous year which confirmed that I was, in many ways, the same bound pastor I had been when serving under Mike. Like the Israelites, I had come out of Egypt, but Egypt had not come out of me.

For example, I felt perfectly justified in pointing out the wrongs committed in my previous church, but was I truly any different? My methods of pastoring the church were painfully close to Mike's methods in too many ways. I still viewed people as sheep who could not make important decisions without the expertise of their shepherd, which of course was me. I expected subservience from those under me. It was annoying to my ego when people did not address me with the title, "Pastor," but instead opted to call me by my first name. Jesus warned against such an attitude in Matthew 23:8-10: "But you are not to be called 'Rabbi,' for you have only one Master and you are all brothers. And do not call anyone on earth 'father,' for you have one Father, and he is in heaven. Nor are you to be called 'teacher,' for you have one teacher, the Christ."

Christ was not condemning the identification of one's particular gift, but I idolized that title to gain preeminence among the brethren.

Through prayer and interacting with close friends, it became clear to me that I was just as insecure as my former pastor had been. I still became angry when other members of "my" church were not dedicated to the vision like I was. I still thought of people as being either "with me" (company players) or "against me" (flakes). How an individual performed according to expectations was my main concern—not that he was a person with needs. I now saw that I was just as much of a villain as I had perceived Mike to be. I encountered the enemy and the enemy was ME!

The church God had sent me to pioneer had the potential of repeating the same mistakes as Good News Chapel. We had enthusiastic and loyal people. We had people committed to serving Christ as Good News Chapel had once had. In fact, this young church appeared to have a pastor who was nearly as isolated as Mike had been. God arrested my attention through this seminar and sent me back to school—the school of the Holy Spirit. He wanted me to relearn what I had evidently missed the first time around. We'll look at one classroom he chose and the teacher he left with me in the next chapter.

As a leader, I thought that my past was distasteful enough to prevent me from repeating the same mistakes—yet here I was doing what I hated to do (Rom. 7:15-20). The more I looked down my nose at the atrocious behavior of my former pastor, the more it became clear that I was exactly like him!

How do you undo years of dysfunctional behavior? The plain truth is that you cannot without repentance. The deception of leaving any cultic church is that you left clean. You didn't. You followed something that was a perversion of the gospel of Christ, and so you therefore must bear the responsibility of sin. If you are committed to blaming everyone else, you will remain hopelessly bound.

Part of my deception was that all I needed in life was God. Most people who are abused by authoritarian leadership consciously or unconsciously believe this erroneous concept. As a result, the only measure they have of right or wrong is their own personal feeling about something or their own understanding of the Scriptures. They presuppose that their vision is accurate and so have already fallen captive to pride.

God had to teach me from the beginning that He is the Truth and that I did not always have all the answers. He began to reveal to me that it was in hearing God through others that freedom would come. I would have to do the very thing my heart was afraid to do: trust.

Those wounded by authority shield themselves from further wounding by erecting a wall of mistrust. One deception is exchanged for another. No, God doesn't want you to return to your former church and submit to error-filled leadership. Yet He does want you to repent toward change. Listen carefully to other Christians who have a close walk with God. Allow them into your life. You may excuse yourself by proclaiming your hurts. You may tell God that you want to hear only from him directly, but all you will hear is a whole lot of silence! If you have ears to hear, learn to hear God through the counsel of others.

I used to preach that God speaks to us through His Word 90 percent of the time and the other 10 percent through prayer and circumstances. While that might seem very comfortable, I have found it to be wrong. God speaks to us about 50 percent of the time through His Word, 30 percent of the time through the sharing and counsel of other Christians, and about 20 percent of the time directly through prayer or circumstantial events. These percentages are changing in my life every day, so don't take these figures exactly.

To allow God to begin to heal what is broken inside, you need to lay aside your insecurity and allow other humans into your life—no more protecting your wounds, no more pretending. God wants to heal you, but he intends to use others to be his messengers.

Consider the case of Philip Peterson. Phil became born-again as a young man. Sensing the call of God upon his life, and under the direction of his pastor, he attended Bible college to train for the ministry. After graduation he assumed the role of associate pastor for a brief time until he was thrust into the role of senior pastor by the moral failure of the church's minister.

During this time period, Phil began to have doubts about the peculiar doctrinal stands of the denomination in which he was serving. These doubts grew into disagreements with home-office representatives. Eventually the denomination that gave Phil his ministry papers exchanged them for his walking papers!

Phil desired to continue in the ministry, but he needed credentials. Through a series of contacts, Phil met Jim Davis, the head of an international ministry called Gospel Center Outreach (GCO). Jim was glad to accept Phil into his fellowship and provide the needed credentials if Phil would agree to take some courses at his Bible school. Phil agreed.

The insecurity he had felt, brought on by the rejection of his former denomination, was replaced with a feeling of security. Now he would be enabled to continue in the ministry God had called him to without further hindrances—or so he thought. Phil met other brothers in the fellowship and being new, began to notice that Jim's organization did some things entirely different from the way in which he had been accustomed.

Phil noticed, for example, that a phenomenal amount of attention was focused on Jim. Virtually every piece of written material talked about what Jim was doing, and how fabulous the ministry was, but little of it seemed to even mention Jesus and his atoning work. He also noticed that his fellow ministers emphasized pastoral authority constantly.

As weeks became months and Phil became acclimated to this new environment, he found himself accepting things he never would have accepted before. Then a chain of events began sounding alarms in Phil's heart, but now all of his friends were also part of the leadership of Gospel Center Outreach.

One day, Frank (Phil's close friend) was ejected from the organization. Letters were written from Jim to members of his church listing slanderous charges. The effect on Frank's church was devastating. People not even familiar with GCO were in turmoil, attempting to reason whose side of the story was accurate. Other ministers on staff at GCO chimed in with Jim's assertions, but Phil knew that the charges just did not make sense. He decided to continue fellowshipping with his old friend, and subsequently he began to know the wrath of Jim Davis.

It wasn't long before Phil received a call. Jim would be coming to his church to minister. Phil had already scheduled a speaker for that particular morning. Jim told him to cancel. Phil was not permitted to question why (but he did—inside at least). Humiliating experiences like this forced Phil to assess many of the strange practices of GCO and its founder. Among other things, he considered the way that ministers of GCO all jockeyed to gain the privilege of sitting next to Jim on the platform during evangelistic meetings; how ministers seemed to look, act, and do things exactly like Jim; the way church members were constantly doing menial chores in and around Jim's residence (yet he did no manual labor—almost as if everyone else was required to be a servant except him); the curious way that Jim intimidated those who challenged him, yelling them down with slanderous criticisms, but then finding a way to restore them upon their acknowledgment that they needed him; the way everyone who didn't do things according to Jim's wishes was labeled "rebellious." By using this method, people were being treated like animals who needed behavior modification to make them obey.

Phil decided to pull the plug soon after he was able to verify through former members and other mitigating circumstances that Jim had been and was continuing to be a practicing homosexual. He confronted Jim in the presence of the other leaders in GCO. Phil was maligned vehemently by Jim and the other pastors. "Who was he," they asked, to oppose "the apostle." Later, when they were alone, Jim offered Phil a secure salary for life if he would keep his church under GCO's oversight! Could it be possible that Jim was stooping to such an outrageous tactic as bribery? Phil resigned.

He soon discovered, as I had, there is no easy way to leave a church into which you have invested your life. There was much pain and inner turmoil to go through. Phil found that the psychological damage he experienced at GCO was the most difficult experience he had to go through. Not only he, but his family had been damaged—maybe for life.

He found it tough to reconnect with his heavenly Father. His mind was a mishmash of Christian doctrine and the traditions of men. Phil struggled to mentally separate the real God from the false one represented by his former leader. The god of GCO was always unreachable and dependent upon right relationship with the leader. Somewhere, deep down, Phil knew that the God who saved him was a God of righteousness, grace, and peace.

Phil found others who had gone through similar experiences. He would spend hours talking with them and comparing notes. It was difficult at first to interact with other ministers. GCO had trained its ministers to feel that they were above other ministers of the gospel. Now, he needed to consider them as brothers in the Lord. Phil's four-year nightmare was over, but the process of rebuilding had only begun.

Years later, after establishing a large and effective church, he began having problems with the leaders he had raised up. Though they loved him, there were too many problems cropping up that looked more like GCO than like the church of Jesus. Phil had honestly thought that the whole ordeal was behind him and "under the blood." In God's eyes, all was certainly forgiven and forgotten, but the patterns Phil learned at GCO needed to be recognized and repented of.

Thankfully, Phil reached out to friends. Rather than running away and denying what his leaders were seeing, he chose to humble himself and ask them for help. He chose the way of humility, and that path always brings grace and subsequent power from God. His grace is sufficient to rescue us when we recommit ourselves to the simple biblical principle of humility.

Coming out of a church that has developed cultic tendencies is difficult at best. Few books are written explaining "how to do it." Those of us who do exit need Christian friends to share with and to whom we can pose questions. During my time serving as a pastor under Mike, he had continually emphasized that Christian leaders cannot be friends with those they lead. That concept would become a horrible bondage to both Mike and the rest of us. He had accepted this idea from some other misguided leader, and we all suffered for it. One of Satan's cleverest devices is to deceive us into cutting ourselves off from God's avenues of counsel. If we are afraid to talk to the people God has ordained to help us, we'll never hear what God wants to say to us through them.

Jesus told his followers, ". . . you are my friends . . . " (John 15:14). Furthermore, Jesus was always making friends. His accessibility was such that children would spontaneously run to him in the middle of his sermons. He ate with people, listened to them, and enjoyed the company of the common Israelite. Think about the sort of approachability Jesus had with the disciples. They even felt free to give him advice! The disciples once advised him how to handle a crowd of five thousand hungry followers (Luke 9:12). Peter felt comfortable enough to counsel him to avoid the cross (Matt. 16:22)! In many cases, the advice was bad; yet, the disciples felt close to Jesus because he regularly shared himself with them.

Mike was a victim of wrong teaching. His beliefs about friendship and what a pastor should be to his congregation chained him to a leadership style that brought him fear and loneliness rather than personal joy and satisfaction. Those under his leadership reaped the same results. We followed his lead and saw our own spiritual lives become weak and ineffective. We became plagued with the same loneliness and frustration. Without nurturing friendships inside or outside our local church, we became as spiritually unbalanced as Mike, and our suffering was in turn passed on to those in our care.

With the revelation that I had left the church, but it had not left me, together with the support of good friends, God began to peel away the layers of false ideas that had built up over the years. I learned that God wasn't as concerned with what abuses I had suffered, as much as what had allowed me to become deceived in the first place. If God didn't address the cause of my being attracted to that deception, I would eventually be trapped again.

When the children of Israel were delivered from the bondage of Egypt, God sovereignly arranged circumstances in their lives to prepare them for what lay ahead. Each test in the wilderness was designed to remove the influence of Egypt from both the way they thought and the way they did things. The tests were painful, but were intended to mold them into warriors who would be fully capable of conquering Canaan. As it turned out, only two of the original group responded correctly to the changes God was attempting to bring about in their lives.

The lesson we can learn from all of this is clear: God does not allow people who are still mentally and spiritually enslaved to inherit his promised land. You and I are no different. The Holy Spirit will use various circumstances and events to help us renew both our thinking and our methods so that they conform to his thinking and his methods. There is simply no way God will permit his people to fully experience the peace of being in his perfect will without responding to the tests he has put into motion for our benefit. We are to respond to the intrusions he allows in our lives with the trust of a child, for "of such is the kingdom of heaven."

Chapter 7

FORE!

"Like a fluttering sparrow or a darting swallow, an undeserved curse does not come to rest" (Prov. 26:2).

Scripture makes it clear that a curse does not just appear arbitrarily. There is a reason it comes. The curse of deception came into my life because of a cause-and-effect relationship. It is not that God decided while I was on Heaven's drawing board, "Casey, you will be part of a church that will become cultic." His perfect will was not that the life that He initiated in me should be perverted and destroyed. God was not the agent of that. The wonder is that our God does take this portion of our lives, which we surrender to him, and forms it just as if it was his divine plan all along.

I fell into deception for reasons that I must take responsibility for. God didn't lead me there; Casey did. A bit more history will help you to understand more clearly what I am trying to say.

My father grew up during the Great Depression. Times were tough outside the home, but worse inside. My father and his father had no father-son relationship. Their home was a battlefield of bitterness, with arguments in no short supply. As a result, he grew up with a strong sense of survival and intensity. His focus was easy to define: Never be poor again. Never raise a family as his father had.

My father reached his goals—sort of. He became a successful business man and, with his childhood sweetheart, raised a family of five boys and one girl. True to his objectives, he didn't treat us the same way his father had treated him. The irony of all ironies, however, was that with the exception of one child, all grew up with varying degrees of bitterness toward him. Though he had conquered poverty, which had brought shame and embarrassment to his own family, the unhealed relationship he had with his own father passed through to most of his own children.

If I had been that one unembittered child, this book would not have been written. But I was one of the other five, and more than that, I was the most bitter of the batch. Though I never engaged in serious drinking or drug abuse, my father often questioned whether I would live to reach my eighteenth birthday. My bitterness expressed itself in total disobedience to his authority. If my father said "black," I replied, "white." I say quite ashamedly now that I hated both of my parents. I was a powder keg looking for a match to self-destruct.

When Jesus found me, I was seventeen-years-old and not the friendliest guy you would ever want to meet. I could count my friends on half of one hand. Yet by his grace, and through the love of Christians, I received him into my life.

People testify as to what happened when they accepted Christ. Some felt burdens lift, angels sing; each account is unique. Mine was rather simple. I immediately noticed upon receiving Jesus that the hate was gone! Because it had been a part of my life, I really did feel as if 50 pounds of flab had been surgically removed.

My father, upon hearing of my conversion, was overjoyed and mystified—overjoyed that the course of my life was no longer on self-destruct, mystified that I would choose to be a Christian of my own free will! When he first saw me after my conversion, he witnessed the change in my entire countenance. There was no hate. In fact, there was love—a love that came from God and extended out through me.

After knowing Christ for only a month, I joined Good News Chapel. Good News Chapel was made up of former rebels like me. Though Christ had cleansed me through his redemptive blood, from the bitterness I had held against my parents, the habitual pattern of resisting authority had not been dealt with scripturally. Even though I no longer hated my father, it was time to establish new patterns built upon God's love in me for him. Practical steps to form a new relationship were what I needed now. I needed someone to take me aside and teach me how to love and honor both my parents as God would have me do.

Good News Chapel was not equipped to train rebels, since Mike was a bit of a rebel himself. Though I no longer hated my father, I learned how Christianity could be used, in effect, to scorn him. I felt justified looking down my nose at my father as a "pagan." Did I preach to both my parents? A lot! But when they didn't respond as expected, I simply wrote them off in my mind.

The seventies were a time when rebellion against parents was in vogue. (I am not sure that much has changed!) Authority was ridiculed rather than honored as God commands. We were young and naive, serving under a man who was struggling through some of his own authority problems. These ingredients combined to create the perfect environment for deception. It may very well be that Satan kept his hands off of our ministry during its early years, knowing that once we had gained a reputation, he could pull the rug out from underneath us using our own folly as his most potent weapon.

Upon leaving Good News Chapel years later, the Holy Spirit began to reprove my cavalier attitude toward my parents through the Scriptures and the counsel of good friends. I came to realize that I needed to start initiating times together with my father.

Our first was a ski trip. My dad agreed to go, but didn't know what to make of it. Why was his son asking him to go anywhere? I had never valued time together with him before. What was son number 3 up to? What I was up to was seeing if God would begin to restore those wasted years of what should have been a good father-son relationship.

On our second such trip, during the Christmas season, my father and I had some long discussions. I decided to hold nothing back of the negative experiences I had while belonging to Good News Chapel. I wanted to give my father access to me, with no hidden agenda. To my surprise, he reciprocated.

At the end of that trip, over a dinner of fresh fish, he delivered a knock-out blow. He said, "You know, I never liked you as a kid growing up, but after today, I want to tell you that I really love you."

What do you say to that? "Pass the ketchup please?" That was the beginning of a process through which rebellion's grip over me was being broken.

Soon after, and knowing my father's avid love of golf, I decided to learn how to play. (I am not sure that ever actually occurred!) Judging from the look on my father's face, I thought he had seen a vision of angels. Within minutes he provided access to a set of clubs and lessons from his golf pro.

Over the next few months and now years, father and son have grown to be much closer through the catalyst of golf. My father and I went out to play one beautiful day at a course designed for serious golfers. Our habit was to play nine without a cart, using the game for exercise and a chance to converse. Even though I was still new to the game, after the first few holes, I was pretty impressed with my game. Then came the next four holes. I scored a twelve on hole six, a ten on hole seven—it did not get better. By the game's end, I was looking forward to just throwing the bags in the car and heading out for a bite to eat.

My father was not so inclined. "Bring your pitching wedge, and let's go to the practice green," he said.

He might as well have said, "Come with me to the Tower of London. I'd like to offer you a haircut." Needless to say, I had no desire to comply, but I followed anyway.

My father's teaching method was simple: I would stay at that green until my golfing skills improved. I needed to follow his instructions exactly, or suffer "constructive" criticism until I did. To most people, that would not seem like a big deal. To me, it was pure pain.

For the next half-hour, he watched every move I made. Whenever I didn't follow instructions, he would let me know in no uncertain terms. His objective was perfectly noble. As a father, he didn't want to see his son lose unnecessary strokes on the golf course. It was on the chipping green that rebellion against authority was exposed in all its ugliness. By my recollection, I had never followed my father's advice one day of my life. I had never honored either of my parents growing up. This fourth of God's commandments had never been observed throughout my thirty-four years.

On this occasion, I determined before God to learn from my father, whether I liked it or not. In effect, I determined to grow up and listen to counsel regardless of how it was given or who it came from. Rebellion against God's authority was the issue that God committed himself to deal with in my heart during this sunny afternoon, and my dad was to be his designated vessel. While rebellion cannot be cured, it can be broken as a controlling force in a person's life. After a half hour of instruction, I learned to chip better and keep my mouth shut. Both were considered monumental achievements! I walked off the golf course that day a changed man.

To bring everything you have read so far into focus, falling into deception is natural to those who are wrongly related to authority. We don't have a cult problem—we have a relationship-to-authority problem. Like the son who leaves home to join the Marines because he doesn't want to listen to mom and dad, only to learn how easy he had it at home, God delivers those who resist his earthly authorities into the hands of tougher authorities. If you think it through, one chief characteristic of churches that go bad is over-authoritative leadership. Who responds to this type of people best? People who have never rightly dealt with God-ordained authority! We live in a country where the majority of children are raised in dysfunctional families. The father is gone, alcoholic, or self-absorbed, showing little interest in the children. Mothers have learned from our society that being a homemaker means accepting a job "beneath" them. Women are pursuing their own identities while the children grow up disconnected from their authorities. What is the result? When they become Christians, they unwittingly begin seeking a surrogate "daddy" in their spiritual leaders.

One man who has done outstanding work in helping people to deal biblically with bitterness and our relationship to God's authorities is Bill Gothard. His *Basic Life Principles* seminars over the last twenty-five or more years have been aimed at dealing with these problems in depth. I do not know of any other ministry that is so greatly used of God to bring the scriptural truths of authority and proper family relationships to people. It was at a *Basic* seminar that I saw clearly what bitterness had done to my life, and what it presently does to those around me. I could fill up several chapters explaining how application of the principles I learned in this seminar caused powerful changes to come about in both the family in which I grew up and the family I now lead.

To get to the point: the reason I was open to deception—even after accepting Jesus Christ as Lord and Savior—was my natural tendency to resist or rebel against the authorities God had originally placed in my life. In my case, that authority was my father. As far as God is concerned, our reaction to any authority is just as important as how right or wrong that authority is. The Scriptures direct us to appeal processes for dealing with abusive authority. We might even reach a point of disobeying such authorities if all appeals are subsequently exhausted. The principle underlying this chapter, however, is that rebellion against God-ordained authority steers men and women toward manipulation and cultic abuse as they go on to form relationships in life.

But what constitutes rebellion? The *American Heritage Dictionary* defines *rebellion* as "an uprising or organized opposition intended to change or overthrow an existing government or ruling authority; an act or show of defiance toward an authority or established convention."

From the above definition, we are led to conclude that rebellion is an outward act of disobedience generated from an inward heart condition of deep resistance. Coincidentally, justified confrontation of ungodly authority might be defined exactly the same way! Both groups refuse to obey authority, yet God rejects one and blesses the other.

A key to helping us further define this word is revealed for us in the Old Testament. The root word for *rebellion* in the Hebrew language is *marah*, which means "bitterness." A rebellious person resists those in authority because he is bitter against authority in general. He does not want to defer to the commands of someone over him. We see this attitude abundantly in every strata of society as millions of people daily engage in criticizing and complaining about those people God has appointed to direct certain areas of their lives. Parents, employers, government officials, teachers, and others with varying degrees of jurisdiction are the regular targets of verbal barbs, jokes, and complaints from people bitter about having to submit themselves to another person.

Challenging authority is not in and of itself rebellion. We would not call Paul the apostle rebellious for confronting Peter, yet he "opposed him to his face" (Gal. 2:11). This was not an exchange of social niceties! Rebuke is a valid form of correcting brothers and sisters (Luke 17:3) and cannot always be viewed as an act of rebellion. The motive for resistance occupies a large portion of whether an individual act is rebellion or justifiable resistance. The method used to enact such resistance occupies the remaining portion. Defiance based upon bitterness incurs God's wrath. Resistance based upon conscience toward God incurs God's protection and blessing.

In Christian circles, we tend to maximize sins such as adultery, lying, stealing, and murder. Rebellion against God-ordained authority is often minimized, if not altogether ignored, as sin.

The Scriptures teach that rebellion is equal to witchcraft in God's eyes, and stubbornness like as iniquity and idolatry (1 Sam. 15:23). The consequence of these practices is alienation from God for he "opposes the proud, but gives grace to the humble" (James 4:6).

My resistance to my father's authority growing up was based solely on bitterness. It had nothing to do with him and everything to do with me. When this revelation became clear, I was forever freed from being duped by illegitimate spiritual authority again.

To break the tendency of being attracted to cultic leadership, you must actively restore those relationships with the authorities God gave to be over you. Naturally, as an adult, you are not still subject to your parents in the way a child is, but you are still responsible during their lifetime to honor them as the fourth commandment instructs. As long as you have it within your power, you must deal properly with whatever authorities God has placed over you, or be condemned to repeat the same cycle of falling headlong into one deception and painful experience after another. When the person in question is deceased, it is still vital that we make things right with our heavenly Father who gave them to be an authority in our life.

Many can point to various "natural" reasons that made them feel obliged to stay in their church: other family members, belief that things would turn around, love for the pastor, and so on. While these and other excuses seem reasonable from a human standpoint, and permit others to develop sympathetic understanding for people in this predicament, they, nonetheless, distract attention from getting to root causes.

As I have shared, my path out of Good News Chapel came to a conclusion when I realized that personal rebellion against God-appointed authority was what attracted me there in the first place. If I ended it there, we could all assume that the way out of any cultic situation is to get right with those authorities that God has placed over your life—and that isn't a bad start! Yet, we need to go deeper.

Rebellion was in the heart of Lucifer when he marshaled one third of the angels to combat the forces of God. He desired preeminence among all other angels and total equality with God. We know that he failed, and as a result was thrust out of heaven.

Now named Satan, or "accuser," he entered human history at its inception with a brilliant strategic maneuver. When he finished with Adam and Eve, he secured for himself the "right" to afflict mankind. By submitting their wills to him and rejecting God's commands, Adam and Eve empowered the devil with the legal right to rule in the affairs of mankind.

Jesus Christ's work at the cross was designed by God as both the solution and an exchange. By asking him to wash away our sins with his blood, and believing he has done what we have asked, our sins are exchanged for his righteousness. One meaning of the phrase, "*born again*," is *to return to the way it was at the beginning*—before Adam and Eve sinned. Satan's "right" to dominate and influence our lives is nullified at salvation. Christ becomes Lord, and Satan's claims to us are broken.

Though this is what God does for us through the cross of Christ, there is yet one important variable that remains: our freedom of will. Satan may have lost exclusive possession of our souls, but his strategies do not cease to be exercised against us. In fact, I believe that his strategies actually intensify against the Christian, since he is now dealing with an adversary who is aware of his goals. Those outside of Christ look upon him as either a mischievous angel who wants to have fun, or a nebulous evil force, which no one can discern or resist. These perceptions in themselves strengthen his ability to influence and destroy lives.

Satan has declared total warfare against God and his servants (Eph. 6:12). Accordingly, he positions himself to gain advantage of the Christian at the least sign of disobedience or independence from God. He knows that so long as believers are in a right relationship with the Father, he has no hope of victory. If he can coax a Christian away from God's protection, he will win easily.

As I clung to rebellion against legitimate authority, Satan was busy building strongholds in my mind. It is in our thinking that he attempts to establish his ideas, which could effectively be called "beachheads." When this occurs, the disciple of Christ is neutralized.

The New Testament declares that we are in a battle from which we will not escape until we physically die. This battle is against the "principalities and powers" of the devil. The primary arena in which this battle takes place daily is our minds.

> The weapons we fight with are not the weapons of the world. On the contrary, they have divine power to demolish strongholds.

We demolish arguments and every pretension that sets itself up against the knowledge of God, and we take captive every thought to make it obedient to Christ (2 Cor. 10:4,5).

The strongholds highlighted in the passage of Scripture above are thoughts. Wrong thoughts can be introduced into our thinking by misguided people, by media, by emotional reactions to circumstances, or by the devil. In the case of the latter, any thought that is left in our thinking processes without being challenged has the opportunity to grow in influence until it becomes an action. Actions that are repeated become habits. Habits that are repeated become life-styles.

As an example, let us consider the average smoker. Such an individual wasn't born with a smokestack in his head. There is nothing in nature that stimulates us to smoke cigarettes. A person smokes to be accepted by other smokers. Peer pressure has everything to do with this disgusting habit.

The potential smoker thinks: "I will try a cigarette, and then others will accept me. I will be part of the 'in-crowd.'" He puts his thought into action by smoking his first cigarette, coughing until he is blue. Then he lights up another. Before long, he is not smoking because he truly wants to, but instead, because he is drawn to the cigarette by addiction. He now has a smoking habit. As time goes on, cigarettes are an identifiable part of who he is. Whenever you interact with him, you must deal with his habit. His breath and clothing tell those who never met him that he is a smoker.

A stronghold develops as we accept and then act upon thoughts inspired by Satan to destroy us. He doesn't "make" us do anything. We choose to accept wrong thinking, and before long this "thinking" can actually prevent us from receiving truth.

We need to understand that people can be bound by religious strongholds as well. All of us have probably experienced the rejection of those who insist that they ". . . don't wish to hear about Jesus," since they, "already have their own church." Out of fear or tradition, people erect walls in their minds to keep from hearing something that might threaten their religious comfort zone.

This stronghold of deception is a fortress built in the mind and reinforced by Satan. Any attempt to introduce the affected person to truth is met with a seemingly tape-recorded message: "I have my own church, "or "I worship God at home," or "I believe my own way."

You can show intelligent Jehovah's Witnesses from their own translation of the Bible Scriptures exactly contrary to their own doctrine, and they will refuse to see it.

A good friend of mine had an experience which illustrates this point well. My friend (himself an ex-Jehovah's Witness) allowed a Jehovah's Witness into his home. Knowing their peculiar doctrines, he began to question this woman about the "great crowd" on earth. (The Jehovah's Witnesses put a lot of emphasis in there being two classes of Christians in heaven. They do not believe that they themselves will go to heaven but, rather that they will be part of "the great crowd" on earth.) He then asked her to read Revelation 19:1 from her own translation of the Bible regarding the location of the great crowd of believers. In this Scripture, it talks about this "great crowd" being in heaven.

When she read the Scripture aloud, he then asked her to tell him where the great crowd was. She responded, "on earth." He then asked her to read it again, asked the same question again, and received the same answer. Here she was reading Scripture out loud which clearly stated that the "great crowd" was in heaven, yet every time she was asked where it was, she replied, "on earth." Exasperated, she finally exclaimed that what the Scripture stated was not what it actually meant. She went further to say that Jehovah's Witness leaders in Brooklyn, N.Y., understood the full meaning of the passages, and she was sure that their interpretation was correct!

Through acceptance of a false religion, in this woman's mind was a stronghold for Satan. When she came into the arena of truth, a wall or stronghold went up preventing her from thinking through what the Scripture plainly says. This wall was built of lies and half-truths, which she was deceived into accepting as reality.

Do not think that leaving a cultic church is the end of your journey. In many cases, there are strongholds of various sizes that are still in place. They are formidable and have no intention of disappearing. Satan would like nothing better than for you to walk away from a church that has gone bad and think you have been delivered from all difficulty. As long as his thoughts are still buried in your mind, he can continue to influence your attitudes, decisions, and will to self-destruct in the future.

For example: How was it that you and I were able to ignore the Holy Spirit's prompting for so long? You can be sure that he was not silent as we spent our time in churches that rejected his lordship. The strongholds, which Satan used on us, were rationalizations that have no more to do with the real issues than stating what church you go to answers the question of whether or not you have a personal relationship with God.

While still at Good News Chapel, I was regularly confronted by others who were not members with the cult-like behavior of both my pastor and myself. Inner walls would go up along with effective defenses in the form of arguments designed to neutralize truth before it could reach my mind or heart. For years, parents, family members, and other Christians questioned our policies, but I never heard what they were saying. Like the Jehovah's Witness mentioned earlier, a stronghold had been built in my mind—and I allowed it to be built there. I would defend our church and our actions, repeatedly denying that we were going the wrong way. I was a Christian, but I was dominated by Satan's influences, allowed in through rebellion.

For those of us who have escaped such groups, we usually were brought to our decision to leave by a crisis. In a way of his choosing, the spirit of God in his mercy enabled us to clearly see how the practices of our former church were not working.

Jehovah's Witnesses often reach this crisis when faced with the dilemma of letting a family member die rather than receive a forbidden blood transfusion. This crisis "jump-starts" the cult member's awareness, which helps them toward rethinking what they believe.

People who leave cultic churches must destroy the strong-holds that Satan was permitted to erect in their thought lives. You were the one who permitted him to do it, so guess what? That's right. You must be the one who now throws down the strongholds he has been using as his headquarters.

Scripture states: "A wise man attacks the city of the mighty and pulls down the stronghold in which they trust" (Prov. 21:22). To pull down a stronghold takes wisdom. Fervor and zeal will not break Satan's footholds. Such efforts are laughable to him at best. To begin the process of defeating him, we must start with personal and sincere repentance. We must admit wrongdoing, for that is how Satan was allowed to build his strongholds in our minds to begin with. Repentance clears our conscience and restores complete fellowship with the Father. I John 1:9 states that we are continually being cleansed by his blood, as we confess our sins to God.

In any battle, one must discover the enemy's strength. The power of Satan to keep you bound is helping you hold onto bitterness, rebellion, anger, stubbornness, and fear. A wise man attacks the enemy by repentance, which removes his strength over our lives.

The next step in this process is to renounce Satan's mental strongholds and to pull them down. "The weapons we fight with . . . have divine power to demolish strongholds. We de-molish arguments and every pretension that sets itself up against the knowledge of God, and we take captive every thought to make it obedient to Christ" (1 Cor. 10:4,5). I believe it is impor-tant that we verbalize each area of rebellion and disobedience, so that God, ourselves, and Satan are sure of our directional intent. We must proclaim Jesus as Lord of our lives and com-mand Satan's forces to pack up and leave.

In doing so, the final step in this sequence is to offer God thanksgiving and praise for hearing our cry and invite him to permanently inhabit these areas of our minds where we previ-ously entertained rebellion and disobedience.

Of course, it goes without saying that this warfare has now begun, not ended. In the hours, days, weeks, and months ahead, you will have to continue to resist the enemy's temptations to go back to the old way of thinking. Willful disobedience must be replaced by willful submission to the Word of God. Rebellion must be replaced with a humble, servant's heart. Repentance and leaning hard upon God's promises ensure that these strongholds will never again be permitted to prejudice our thinking and lead us into bondage again. ". . . The one who is in you is greater than the one who is in the world" (1 John 4:4).

Chapter 8

WHAT DOES A "PERFECT" CHURCH LOOK LIKE, ANYWAY?

My desire in sharing this book with you is to help you to spiritual health. After you have biblically (and thus effectively) dealt with the past, finding a new church may be a part of the process in your particular situation. So how do you do that? The Bible doesn't tell you to go to one church in particular, yet we know that God would have you to be an active part of a local expression of the body of Christ.

When there are humans involved, a perfect church is unlikely. Most of us, if we are honest, don't really want a perfect church. We would be intimidated by a fellowship that always did everything exactly right in all circumstances all the time. What most of us long for is a church where we feel intimately involved in its vision, a place where leadership listens and values our input.

I am not an anarchist. Genuine church authority is a wonderful blessing from our Father. Do not err by concluding that church authority is bad, for that has not been what I have written, nor would I like this book to achieve such a negative goal. My task as a spiritual surgeon has been to make incisions into suffering Christians so that dangerous diseases can be both identified and removed. As with any operation, a surgeon's function is not complete until the patient has been sutured back up to allow the total healing to take place. With this in mind, I would now like to briefly discuss some principles of church government and authority for you to consider. It is not my intention to force my beliefs upon you, nor to state that these ideas are the only way churches should function. I speak as someone who has, shall we say, "been around."

I believe that church government and authority follows the "Sabbath" principle. Jesus stated that "the Sabbath was made for man, not man for the Sabbath." The scribes and Pharisees had bound people to thousands of little laws. They lived in constant fear of violating the Sabbath, which would dishonor Jehovah. They made a "god" out of the Sabbath itself and completely missed the intent God had in establishing it. Jesus corrected their trivial emphasis by saying in effect, "The Sabbath was made to set men free in their relationship to God, not bind them up with petty laws of men" (Mark 2:27; my paraphrase). God's intent was to bless men, not burden them.

Church government and the authority God empowers it with were given to enhance man's relationship to God, not make him an obedient servant of a power-based leadership. Government was made for man, not man for government. How do individuals become church pastors in today's church? Usually, the following criteria are generally accepted as workable:

- a personal call into ministry, subjectively sensed by the individual, who is able to clearly articulate such a call;
- verification of such a call by other proven church leaders beginning with the pastor; such leaders also examine the candidate to see that the requirements of I Timothy 3:1-7 are met;
- some sort of training or mentoring process (in many cases seminary or Bible school);
- the ordination of the candidate; this is a public recognition by other leaders that the person has been authorized by God to serve in such a function.

In many cases, graduates from Bible school or seminaries go through some sort of candidating procedure. A number of things are involved in this process:

- the congregation a candidate has interest in serving hears him preach a few times and gets a sense of whether he fits their expectation;
- the candidate is questioned on matters of doctrine to determine if "his" fits "theirs";
- references from the training institution are sought and examined;
- conversations with those who have a first hand knowledge of the candidate's Christian experience and character are often pursued to get a clearer picture of the candidate in action.

Please understand: there is no absolute process that the Bible demands. These ideas represent permissible method. No Scripture is against using this process, but neither does it enforce these as the only guidelines through which individuals become pastors. Whatever the process, the true verification of a person's call to minister comes from God, and that will become evident over time spent actually doing the work of ministry.

The idea of ordaining persons into ministry is derived from Titus 1:5 and other passages, where Paul instructed his leaders to appoint or ordain elders in each town. With this leadership came authority, which means the power to act on God's behalf (Acts 14:5; 20:28; 1 Tim. 5:17).

With this privilege comes the responsibility to be accountable. Leaders are chosen on the basis of character (1 Tim. 3:1-7). High standards of personal and moral conduct are expected for those who serve as leaders (Deut. 7:16-20; 2 Sam. 12:13,14; Matt. 23:1-35). Those who do fulfill scriptural requirements are worthy of our respect and support (Rom. 13:6,7).

Legitimate leadership is a calling to be a servant, not a lord (Matt. 20:20-28; 1 Pet. 5:2,3). Understanding this concept is where the trouble usually begins. In these Scriptures, Jesus and Peter emphasize the "servanthood" of leadership. In II Timothy 4:2, Titus 1:10-13, and Hebrews 13:17, the "authority" of leadership is highlighted. This paradox is what American churches don't seem to comprehend. Pastors and church leaders are commissioned to lead by diving under those who follow them. Authority is given by God, but it becomes effective among the flock through serving and humility.

The Pastor-Controlled Church

One of the most perplexing problems today's church faces, in my opinion, is the "pastor-controlled" church. With the authority God has invested into leaders, some pastors have easily accepted the notion that exercising authority means they are "closer to God" than others in the congregation. As a result, a type of class system develops in which those exercising authority are elevated to positions God never intended.

In the business world, one's self-esteem rises with the increase of power over others. The acquisition of office space, furniture, special privileges, and the like denote the ever-increasing value an employee has to a company. Some churches have mistakenly bought into that same concept by making the pastoral gift more important than others. A pastor may have more visibility, but God does not "measure" the importance of gifts. They are all needed and all valuable. Paul's discourse in I Corinthians 12 bears this out.

> Now the body is not made up of one part, but of many.
>
> If the foot should say, "Because I am not a hand, I do not belong to the body," it would not for that reason cease to be part of the body.
>
> And if the ear should say, "Because I am not an eye, I do not belong to the body," it would not for that reason cease to be part of the body.
>
> If the whole body were an eye, where would the sense of hearing be? If the whole body were an ear, where would the sense of smell be?
>
> But in fact, God has arranged the parts in the body, every one of them, just as he wanted them to be (1 Cor. 12:14-18).

Being a pastor is, in essence, a gift. As such, it was not earned as in the business world. Pastors are graced with a gift that is designed for specific purposes. In some churches, we have expected the pastor to operate as elder, apostle, prophet, evangelist, teacher, and administrator simultaneously. This is wrong. The gift of being a pastor builds off the shepherd model and the father model. A pastor leads and guides like a spiritual father.

A closer look at the New Testament reveals that the five grace-gifts mentioned in Ephesians 4:11 were given to prepare God's people for works of service, so that the body of Christ may be built up until we all reach unity in the faith and in the knowledge of the Son of God and become mature (Eph. 4:12-13). God has assigned at least five gift applications to the specific task of bringing the church to a mature estate. "Pastor" is mentioned for the first and only time in verse 11. These grace-gifts are to function together corporately, helping the church toward maturity.

What is that maturity? "From him (Christ), the whole body, joined and held together by every supporting ligament, grows and builds itself up in love, as each part does its work" (v.16). In other words, the prime directive of apostles, prophets, evangelists, pastors, and teachers is to interact with church members in such a way as will enable them to discover "their" spiritual gifts and competently contribute these gifts toward the welfare of the rest of the body of Christ. Church growth is the natural outcome when this happens. The church functions as a living organism rather than a dead organization.

A facet we see in the early church was the close harmony between apostles and elders in the decision-making processes of the church (See Acts 15:2-16:4). Many born-again churches have rejected the ministries of apostle and prophet by relegating them to the first century. Typical of our ignorance, we build our theology around our failure to understand what these ministries are supposed to be, and how they are intended to operate. Unfortunately, even those churches that claim to believe in these ministries do not appear to have the vaguest inkling as to how to make room for them. And why? Because we believe that the pastor is the vortex through which all power and anointing flows. Other gifts have gotten lost in the shuffle.

The Board-Controlled Church

To prevent pastors from becoming mini-kings, some churches have opted to elect a board to run the church. In this case, the pastor is hired, fired, and monitored, subject to the board's approval. While this model seems safer, it is amazing how many congregations replace power-based pastors with equally power-based boards.

I am aware of churches where pastors work part-time jobs—not because the church lacks sufficient funds, but because of miserly boards. I know of churches where the pastor serves as little more than spiritual custodian, powerless to effect godly change because of the stranglehold that key board members hold over his present and future. Whenever people are permitted to use title or position to enhance their own selfish ambitions, God's spirit is quenched.

The Essence of Church Authority

It would be helpful perhaps if we considered the fact that leadership is a function within the church instead of a title or means of gaining power and recognition. All of us have a function to both discover and fulfill in a local church. God ordains leaders to assist other members to find their calling (Eph. 4:11,12) and direct them toward biblical principles.

Authority is given by God to enhance man's relationship with him. God has authorized the Ephesians 4:11 gifts with great authority. Elders have also been given authority to oversee local church affairs in some cases, but, also, authority over many churches in others (Acts 15:6). In addition, I believe he has given varying degrees of authority to all the gifts mentioned in Romans 14:4-8 as well as I Corinthians 12:8-11.

Any local church is designed by God to be a place where people "plug in" and begin functioning within the gifted areas God has given them. Going into the ministry should not be synonymous with becoming a pastor. Being a pastor is a wonderful gifting—to those who are called to be such. But we need to open ourselves up to other callings, because every leader is gifted in the areas of being a pastor.

Ideally, the church has elders who see to its affairs, protect it from error, and provide accountability for its ministers. The pastor is then released to do just that—pastor! His function would involve counseling, admonishing, encouraging, and training others to see to the personal needs of the flock. A teacher in the same church could assume the oversight of the teaching aspects of church life. It would not mean that the pastor's and teacher's gifts could not overlap, but simply that both gifts would function in the area where they do best. The ultimate objective of these gifts is always to train others to pastor, teach, evangelize, and so on.

Kenneth Mitchell, in his book *Multiple Staff Ministries*, examines various problems he and others have encountered when attempting to learn why some church staffs do not function well. He looks at various models of leadership and concludes his book by discussing the most useful model of our day. It is the person who is willing to take responsibility, who tries to maintain an overview of all the ministries being undertaken in a particular congregation, and who can make sure that the authority necessary to get a particular job done is in the appropriate hands. "Such a person sees herself or himself as a member of the system, one who has particular functions (which include leadership and direction at times), but who does not pretend to embody in his or her own person the total ministry of the church."

Mitchell in effect challenges those who oversee the church not to see themselves as so indispensable that the church will fold without their constant care. God is bigger than that. Frankly, if the church would fall apart without us, we are building something that is not in keeping with God's plan.

Prophets, evangelists, and apostles have been raised up by the Holy Spirit to equip the body of Christ. How many churches truly recognize, discover, equip, and utilize these ministries? We have become so consumed with controlling the church that God's original intent for the integration of all his gifts have been locked out!

Evangelists train the body of Christ to win the lost. We have relegated them to self-contained ministries, which set up in coliseums for a week of meetings. Meanwhile, the local church suffers for lack of vision in reaching the lost. We don't need professional evangelists to do the church's work. Evangelists are gifted to train others to effectively win the unsaved.

Prophets are a hot topic today. God uses them to jolt his church out of its self-satisfaction and tune in to what he is saying. The absence of prophets in past generations has kept the church from being relevant to the needs of a changing society. Prophets speak a *rhema* word from God. They are accountable, just as those with any other gifts, to church authority, but they are vital to our future. Prophets keep the church from majoring on minors. They help the church to focus on what God is currently doing. Apostles function specifically in the raising up of other church leaders. They are gifted by God to gather people together into vibrant church bodies. They are church planters, who raise up local leadership and move on to establish more churches.

Those with the gift of leadership can be put to work in a number of areas. The church always needs servants who are gifted to lead. Administrative gifts are designed to help make certain that other gifted people are released to function in the area to which God has called them. (We don't need people with a gift of intercessory prayer heading up the Sunday School department.)

Men or women who are graced with gifts of healing or miracles need to be encouraged to pray for the sick and be released in outreach evangelism. You can see how the releasing of these gifts would immediately benefit the body of Christ.

Pastors or boards, which have consciously or unconsciously shielded their churches from the influences of these ministries through fear, have cut their congregations off from much of what God is saying to them. Unknowingly, they have made themselves the mediators between God and their members. Is it any wonder so many pastors (or boards) become so isolated and lonely?

Down through the centuries, we have become calcified in our thinking. The patterns from which we have drawn our leadership examples are the churches we have tried to escape. In our efforts to be unlike them, we have used them as our focus to become just like them. The New Testament church is our model to imitate. There we find not only a structure of government, but an essence of it. Having the perfect structure is not the answer. Having a structure that also demonstrates the spirit of cooperation, gentleness, humility, and so on better reflects God's ultimate purposes for church government.

The objective God has in mind is that every human alive has the opportunity to become a disciple of the Lord Jesus. If our church governmental structures make it difficult for people to have access to all that God has created them to be, we need to reexamine them to discover whether they reflect God's heart or the fears and insecurities of men.

I believe in honoring and obeying God's authorities. A church leader's true authority is demonstrated more through his love for God than through acting in a way designed to "keep people in line." Shepherding God's flock involves patience, long-suffering, and many other arduous character traits. The shepherds of Palestine were nobodies who loved caring for helpless animals. It wasn't a job that brought prestige or a great deal of financial gain, but it was a job with which God was pleased to identify himself in Psalm 23.

Church leaders who do a good job are "worthy of double honor . . . " (1 Tim. 5:17). The verses that follow indicate that part of bestowing this honor involves seeing to the financial needs of leaders in a responsible fashion. If there exists a proper love relationship among church leaders, full-time pastoral staff will have the integrity to submit a fair budget proposal, and the elders (or a committee so designated) will have the grace to be understanding and generous.

In the church decision-making process, the wise pastor learns to listen before acting. In Acts 15:13-21 we read that James, who was the leader among the apostles at the time, listened to the input of all the apostles and elders. He then made a decision that reflected God's purposes as expressed through many of them. It is wise to have consensus among other leaders, utilizing as many of the various gifts as possible, so that God's perfect will may be known and carried out.

In the church, the pastor or elders need to initiate access to other gifted members. If there are those with spiritual gifts, the maximum benefit of what God is saying through them should be sought and utilized. Eventually, like James, someone must bear the responsibility of making the decision. However, when there is shared ownership in the decision-making process, there is less risk of being out of sync with God's will. The morale of the church will tend to remain high, because other leaders will know that their voices and gifts count for something. A sense of comradeship will filter down through the rest of the church as well.

In seeking to be part of a church that glorifies God and stands a better chance of serving him over the long haul, look for a ministry where leaders are not afraid of being accountable to the church they are called to serve. Ideally, clear methods of appealing decisions should be in place. If they aren't in place, can they be put in place? Could you be of assistance?

I value leadership in the body of Christ not only because we all should (Heb. 13:17), but because I continue to serve a local church in a pastoral role. It is a function that is at times very difficult, and at other times is very rewarding. Like Paul, however, I must say that leading is not a matter of choosing a good job, but a function I have little choice of refusing, if I want God's will for my life (1 Cor. 9:16)! I have come to cherish times when others inside and outside of my church have challenged decisions I have made out of concern for either myself or the body of Christ. I realize that those who do challenge have gifts and abilities that can help the entire church—if I listen. The elders who serve with me are called to bear the same burden I bear. We are always in a process of learning to make decisions together. Admittedly, I was afraid to do so at first, fearing they would make mistakes. They did! But, so what? I make mistakes, too! Since our focus is to serve our church, the need for personal recognition and ego-stroking is moot. With Christ the sought-after head of operations, our church is much healthier, and we all feel safer, since decision-making does not all rest with one man.

Chapter 9

REPAIRER OF THE BREACH—OR ACCUSER OF THE BRETHREN?

A good friend of mine challenged me recently with this statement: The only difference between the repairer of the breach and the accuser of the brethren is that the repairer goes further with the same information. The accuser chooses to despise those who are in error.

It has been a struggle to be a repairer of the breach. There are so many broken walls that need repair, and criticizing those who hurt the church by their sins is so much easier than praying for their repentance and restoration; yet, that is what God has called us to do. He has been teaching me to address evil when he puts it within my power to do so, but not to despise those bound by that evil. I used to be an abuser and God was merciful to me. Can I do anything less toward those who continue to blindly abuse God's people?

I never cease to be amazed at how God has taken my own experiences and turned them for both His glory and my good. The depression, which engulfed my soul months after leaving Good News Chapel, was difficult to wade through. I was not depressed because I left, but discouraged because I looked back over fourteen years and felt as if my life had been wasted. A significant portion of each day was spent mentally kicking myself for being so foolish that I continued to be part of such a cultic church.

To make matters worse, the further away from Good News Chapel I got, the more clearly I saw how utterly deceived I had been. The more spiritually alert I became, the more embarrassed and depressed I felt for being such a dope.

Today, I do not feel that way at all. Today, I know that God really does work all things together for good. He truly has redeemed those wasted years and made every one of them profitable and valuable, if not altogether a living testimony of what can happen to Christians who fail to pay attention to biblical principles for godly living.

Looking back, I can see now how each negative experience has trained me to be a blessing. I am more aware of what makes churches fail than textbooks could have taught me. I know better how to relate to people caught in the web of cults than any video presentation could have ever shown me. I am more equipped to offer comfort and encouragement to the hundreds who are at this moment struggling with the same issues. Since I left Good News Chapel, God has seen to it that most of my time has been devoted to assisting Christians to either confront or avoid the same cultic patterns in their own lives and ministries.

Too often, much of our time is frittered away by regretting the mistakes of the past. Regret produces nothing but more regret.

Paul the apostle said, ". . . One thing I do: Forgetting what is behind, and straining toward what is ahead, I press on toward the goal to win the prize for which God has called me heavenward in Christ Jesus. All of us who are mature should take such a view of things" (Phil. 3:13-15). From this context, we can deduce that becoming a mature Christian will involve a deliberate "forgetting" of things that didn't go quite right. Why should we determine to forget? Because God's higher goal must be achieved, and we cannot achieve that goal so long as we sit on the sidelines crying over our injuries.

When you examine all that has happened to you in the light of eternity, the time you spent going the wrong way is not really that important. From God's vantage point, he is happy to see you turning around towards him. He is overjoyed to have you back in a loving relationship.

When the thief on the cross turned away from his mistakes to acknowledge Jesus, the Lord didn't scold him for being so stupid as to have gotten himself crucified. He could have justifiably lectured the thief on all the wrongs he had committed. Instead, he promised him a place in paradise. That is the God we serve.

Think about the bargain we got when we came to him for salvation in the first place. "Truly," as Paul states, "not many wise or noble" are in our ranks (1 Cor. 2:6). In reality, God has the misfits of humanity to call his own. We are, by and large, not the sort of people God can be proud of from a natural standpoint—yet he is.

He never complains. God truly loves those who call upon him. He uses the "base things" to confound the wisdom of the mighty, and we are those base things. In fact, he "delights" in us! Psalms 147:11 states: "The Lord delights in those who fear him, who put their hope in his unfailing love." We who have been deceived need to accept that it happened and respond to the changes God wants to make in us now to keep the same thing from occurring again. To do this, our past has to be deliberately placed into the hands of God and released. We cannot afford to hold on to our root as some sort of security blanket . Far too many use their past as a crutch for the present by saying, "I was hurt in the past by committing myself. I will never do that again." The only thing that declaration says is that bitterness has not been dealt with properly.

The truth is: You cannot afford to avoid committing yourself to the local church again. Your mistake was not that you committed yourself, but that you committed yourself to something beyond what God's Word teaches. You erred when you hung on to the form of godliness, when his very presence had long departed. You got hurt when you failed to honor the authorities he blessed you with in your formative years, so take your lumps like everyone else and go on with God!

The reason why we hang on to apprehensions about joining other churches is rooted in fear. Each of us has a need to find acceptance by other people—especially those who exercise some kind of authority. Like it or not, there is a tremendous amount of security in a strong, unaccountable leader. They are strong, deliberate, seemingly courageous individuals who seem to know exactly who they are and where they are going. Many of us are attracted to that because of our own insecurities. There is a certain perverse comfort in allowing a leader to make most of our decisions for us. These are decisions God has commissioned us to make for ourselves. It was aggravating but relatively easy to put your brain in neutral at church and let leadership determine what God's will was or wasn't. Now, you are returning to biblical Christianity, the faith where all men must be responsible for determining what God's will for their lives is—or isn't. This does not mean independence from authority, but proper relationship to it.

Your experiences will either be stumbling blocks, which sideline your Christian faith or stepping stones to where God still intends for you to go. In athletics, there used to be a saying: "No pain, no gain." I do not know any competent Christian who has not experienced gut-wrenching emotional pain at one time or another, if they have been Christians for any length of time. It is not pain that stops you—it is what you do with the pain. Athletes use pain to train and discipline themselves. Those who shrink from pain never win races.

To conclude on a refreshing note, I ask you to recall a saying printed across a poster years ago: "When life gives you lemons, make lemonade!" Real lemonade is one of my favorite summertime drinks. It refreshes with a bite to it that leaves you puckering. Soft drinks are O.K., but their effect is quickly forgotten. Lemonade stays with you, because its tart flavor satiates every taste bud.

I have discovered through our family's experiences that we are not worse off for having gone through the disillusionment of a church gone bad. There is now more of a "bite" to what we do for Christ. Because of these events, I waste little time investing myself in fruitless enterprises. There is within me a keen awareness and discernment for ministries that manipulate people's spiritual lives. I don't regret this new awareness. If He had to use these negative experiences to create this in me, glory to him! I am happy to be where Christ can now utilize these experiences to help others out of the same predicaments, perhaps even while helping me to heal the ones who inflict the wounds if they allow me access.

In writing this book, I realized that I could never hope to accomplish the task of healing every hurt or answering every question you have. What I have attempted to do is give you some principles to think about and apply under God's direction. When the bottom line appears, what really matters is that we as Christians are all brothers and sisters. Loving one another is more a matter of what we do than what we say. Christianity means more than attending church services and doing good deeds. To really live for Christ means being willing to strengthen and help each other to live for Christ as purely as possible. This is my heart's desire, and I hope this book has accomplished that purpose.

NOTES

MORE PRESCOTT PRESS BOOKS

Pinky, The Sow
That Was Washed

by Darlene Saunders
with illustrations by
Brian Norton

Come along and enjoy the summer adventures of twins Brant and Brenda Price. Brant and Brenda experience a whole new world on their grandparent's farm. They even come to enjoy working on the farm and having the chance to bring the spirit of the Lord to their new-found friends and even to their grandparents. *Pinky, The Sow That Was Washed* is a story that your children will thoroughly enjoy!

ISBN#:0-933451-11-3
$5.99 Quality Paper

Satanization of Society

by Robert Rosio
Does evil occur randomly? Does evil personified exist?

Have you ever wondered why our society has started the downward spiral we seem to be in? Is 'secular humanism' or the 'new age' movement the cause of all this turmoil? Robert Rosio, author of *Hitler and the New Age*, has studied the causes of decline in American society and has written an analysis of our current dilemma. Rosio paints a frighteningly graphic portrait of the real 'spirit of the age' that lurks behind the pseudo-spiritualism of the 'new age' movement and secular humanism.

ISBN#:0-933451-26-1
$9.99 Quality Paper

Powers and Princes

by Vaughn Stenis

In this stunning and graphic portrayal of spiritual conflict, Stenis weaves a unique and vivid tapestry of fact and fiction detailing creation, the fall of Lucifer, and the creation of man. With breathtaking woodcuts and classical paintings as illustrations, *Powers and Princes* is a rare jewel. Spanning the centuries from the beginning of time to the death of Jacob in Egypt, *Powers and Princes* is an engagingly new perspective on an age old story.

ISBN#:0-933451-14-8

$9.99 Quality Paper

How Little We Knew

by Dee Miller

When it involves the clergy no one wants to get involved. It's the kind of subject people wish would just go away. Dee Miller, author and mental health nurse, dares to challenge the great perpetuator: SILENCE!

As a professional in the mental health field, Miller reveals her own story of denial about clergy sexual abuse while in the mission field. *How Little We Knew* is a dramatic story exposing clergy abuse and how the system tries to conceal it.

Dee's entire experience uproots her foundation and leaves her faith in shambles!

ISBN#: 0-933451-18-0

$9.99 Quality Paper

Go Ye Into Africa

by Lynn Carol Bowling

Out of the sweltering plains of Africa comes a story of one couple's response to the biblical injunction to "...go ye into all the world..." Bowling chronicles her experiences and trials of the African mission fields. Amid exotic tropical flora, everyday dangers of African wildlife, and restless natives, the author shares her incredible journey and commitment to the realities of living out her faith.

ISBN#: 0-933451-12-1

$9.99 Quality Paper

Two Trees—Two Natures

by Dr. Joel H. Ehrlich

A debate rages in Christian circles today centering around the role of psychology in the church. Some say psychology is a useful tool in gaining necessary insights into understanding how and why we think. Others say it is a secular religion that seeks to subvert and overthrow true Christianity. Is there any middle ground?

Ehrlich is a staunch advocate of true Biblical counseling, which bypasses man-made theories and uses the Word of God as its only authority. In *Two Trees, Two Natures,* Ehrlich exposes the seductiveness of psychology and hopes to equip pastors and laity alike to handle all of life's problems based on God's Word.

ISBN#: 0-933451-24-5

$9.99 Quality Paper

PRESCOTT PRESS
ORDER FORM

Title	Qty.	Price Each	Total
Go Ye Into Africa		$9.99	
How Little We Knew		$9.99	
Pinky, the Sow		$5.99	
Powers and Princes		$9.99	
Satanization of Society		$9.99	
Two Trees, Two Natures		$9.99	
Freedom from Eating Disorders		$9.99	
Freedom from Eating Disorders/wkbk.		$14.99	
When A Church Goes Bad		$6.99	
		Subtotal:	
		Shipping:	
		Total:	

Shipping & Handling:
Please add $3.50 for shipping and handling for the first book, and .50 for each additional book up to 5 books.

Method of Payment:
Please indicate method of payment.
___Check or money order enclosed.
___MasterCard
___VISA
Credit Card#: _____
Expiration Date: _____

Address Package/Mail To:
Name _____
Address _____
City _____ State_____ Zip _____
Phone number _____

Send orders to:
Prescott Press, Inc.
Mail Order Dept.
P.O. Box 53777
Lafayette, LA 70505
1-800-226-7737